David Eldridge

The Knot of the Heart

David Eldridge was born in Romford, Greater London. His
full-length plays include *Serving it Up* (Bush Theatre, 1996); *A
Week with Tony* (Finborough Theatre, 1996); *Summer Begins* (NT
Studio and Donmar Warehouse, 1997); *Falling* (Hampstead
Theatre, 1999); *Under the Blue Sky* (Royal Court Theatre,
2000, awarded the *Time Out* Live Award for Best New Play
in the West End in 2001); *Festen* (Almeida and Lyric Theatre,
2004); *M.A.D.* (Bush Theatre, 2004); *Incomplete and Random
Acts of Kindness* (Royal Court Theatre, 2005); a new version of
Ibsen's *The Wild Duck* (Donmar Warehouse, 2005); *Market Boy*
(National Theatre, 2006); a new version of Ibsen's *John Gabriel
Borkman* (Donmar Warehouse, 2007); *Under the Blue Sky* (Duke
of York'sTheatre, 2008); an adaptation of Jean-Marie Besset's
Babylone (Belgrade Theatre, Coventry, 2009); *A Thousand Stars
Explode in the Sky* co-written with Robert Holman and Simon
Stephens (Lyric Hammersmith, 2010); and a new version of
Ibsen's *The Lady from the Sea* (Royal Exchange Theatre, 2010).

David Eldridge

The Knot of the Heart

Methuen Drama

Methuen Drama

Methuen Drama, an imprint of Bloomsbury Publishing Plc

3 5 7 9 10 8 6 4 2

Methuen Drama
Bloomsbury Publishing Plc
50 Bedford Square
London WC1B 3DP
www.methuendrama.com

Copyright © David Eldridge 2011

David Eldridge has asserted his rights under the Copyright, Designs and
Patents Act 1988 to be identified as the author of this work.

ISBN: 978 1 408 15331 4

A CIP catalogue record for this book is available from the British Library

Available in the USA from Bloomsbury Academic & Professional,
ifth Avenue/3rd Floor, New York, NY 10010. www.BloomsburyAcademicUSA.com

Typeset by DC Graphic Design Ltd, Swanley Village, Kent

The Knot of the Heart

For Dennis, Faye and Mark Eldridge

Presume not that I am the thing I was;
For God doth know, so shall the world perceive,
That I have turn'd away my former self;
So will I those that kept me company.

William Shakespeare, *Henry IV Part 2*

Acknowledgements

I would like to thank all the people who talked to me and encouraged me in the writing of the play: DB and the actors who played so openly in the pre-writing workshop in August 2009; ME for her encouragement and advice; Michael Attenborough and Jenny Worton at the Almeida for their enthusiasm and for backing me to the hilt in what I wanted to write.

Special thanks to everyone who helped me research this play: Peter Woolf, Julie Myerson, Kate McKenzie and Jane Treays; Verity Maidlow, Steve Backshall and Miquita Oliver; Dr Owen Bowden Jones and the special people at Chelsea and Westminster Hospital Drug Treatment Centre; Maria Robinson and all the special people at City Road Crisis Intervention Centre.

And of course Lisa Dillon for whom the role of Lucy has been created, for all the passion and encouragement along the way, and not least for suggesting I might like to write 'a role with a journey like the sort the boys usually get to go on'.

David Eldridge
February 2011

The Knot of the Heart was first performed at the Almeida Theatre, London on 10 March 2011.
The cast, in order of appearance, was as follows:

Lucy	Lisa Dillon
Barbara	Margot Leicester
Zac/Pete/Brian/Dr Harris/	
Andrew/Oscar	Kieran Bew
Angela	Abigail Cruttenden
Marina	Sophie Stanton

Director   Michael Attenborough
Designer   Peter McKintosh
Lighting Designer   Tim Mitchell
Composer and Sound Designer   Dan Jones

Characters

Lucy

Angela

Barbara

Marina

Zac, Pete, Brian, Dr Harris, Andrew and **Oscar** should be played by a single actor.

One

Lucy, *twenty-seven, and her mother* **Barbara**, *sixty, are in the garden of their large Islington home. It's a quiet warm summer's evening.*

Barbara *drinks from a glass of red wine.* **Lucy** *takes an empty Bic Biro from her cardigan pocket and a folded square of tin foil. She unfolds it. Tears some off and wraps it around the Biro to make a tube which she hangs out of her mouth like a cigarette. She replaces the Biro, tears some more foil to make a flat oblong surface and then takes a small lump of heroin out of a small wrap which she puts on that foil.*

Lucy   Will you hold it for me?

Barbara   I know what that is.

Lucy *looks at her mother.*

Lucy   You've never minded me smoking joints in the garden.

Barbara   This is too much Lucy.

Lucy   Mummy I'm twenty-seven. I make my own choices. I do my own thing.

Silence.

Fine when Zac comes down we'll go in Gibson Square. Fuck's sake. Doesn't matter any more anyway.

Barbara   No. Don't. Please darling.

She thinks and then approaches **Lucy**. **Lucy** *passes the foil with the heroin to her mother which she holds.* **Lucy** *finds a Zippo in her pocket which she also passes to her mother.* **Barbara** *ignites the Zippo which she holds underneath the smack.* **Lucy** *smokes it.* **Barbara** *watches her daughter.* **Lucy** *backs away and takes the foil tube from her mouth.*

Lucy   See? I'm still here. Lots of my friends do it. Like no one's injecting or anything. Its only a tiny bit of opium. And I've had such an awful day you wouldn't believe it.

Barbara   Lucy you promised me you would never.

Lucy   I would never inject. I would never do that to you. I would never do to that to myself. I promise. On my life.

She screws the foil into a ball and flicks it away.

Barbara   Oh darling not on the lawn.

She looks for the flicked foil in the garden.

Lucy   What are you doing?

Barbara   It will drive me mad the thought of it in the garden.

Lucy   A bird will carry it away. Or a worm will eat it.

Barbara   How will a worm digest such a thing?

Lucy   Worms love foil.

Barbara   Worms don't love anything darling. They've no feelings or brain.

Lucy   How dare you be so dismissive of the great British worm.

Barbara   Darling believe me I'm a great fan of the worm. I just haven't met one yet that can compost tin foil.

Lucy   They love it. Foil is worm bling.

Barbara   What's bling?

Lucy *laughs and then becomes reflective.*

Lucy   Don't you remember in the pilot last year?

Barbara   What was that darling?

Lucy   Are you listening? On my show.

Barbara   No.

Lucy   We had a whole green school awards thing. And I don't know. This funny little prep school in Bloomsbury had done a project on worms and we had the kids on with their worms. So we did worms. You know it's the kind of stupid shit we do in children's television.

Barbara   Yes, yes.

Lucy   I love it.

Silence.

Barbara   You would tell me if something was wrong?

Silence.

Lucy   The epigeic worm is a bit of a bore but the lob worm is a hard mother-fucker.

Barbara   Lucy.

Lucy   He lives ten feet below the surface and comes up at night for supper. Yes your average epigeic tiger worm hasn't got the balls to even take on a dead fly. But your *Lumbricus terrestris* will eat my little gift in one gulp and buzz its tits off as a prize to boot.

Barbara   I wish I'd known you were coming.

Lucy   Why?

Barbara   Well.

Lucy   Mother chill your boots.

Barbara   I'd have cooked.

Lucy   Oh for God's sake you know how it makes me feel ill to look at such a ridiculously large plate of food. And you expect me to actually eat it. You know Mummy if you want to make me a sandwich, make me a sandwich and let's not keep harping on about it.

Barbara *drinks and studies Lucy.*

Barbara   Okay.

Lucy   Well are you going to make a sandwich?

Barbara   I will in a minute.

Lucy   Well I'll have cheese and jam.

Barbara   Okay.

Lucy   And some crisps.

Barbara   Yes.

She drinks and looks at the garden.

Lucy   You know mummy something's happened.

Barbara   I knew.

Lucy   Did you?

Barbara   I had a feeling. Will you give me a minute darling? Will you just give me a moment? I –

She drinks. Silence.

Barbara   Of course the secret to a truly great bouillabaisse is in the orange peel and fennel seed.

Lucy *warns her mother off with a look.*

Barbara   I'm only saying I would have made a meal. When one thinks of the great hopes I had for this garden when we first came here Lulu. I can remember it like yesterday. In the old two-oh-five with the roof down and you and Angela in the back looking around Gibson Square. And the removals men were already fetching our belongings in. And Grandmother's picture had been broken and you were a darling telling the boy who broke it not to worry when you knew how furious I was. Even at that age. So pretty. Cuddling Mr Dog your favourite.

She drinks.

Barbara   Yes. An arbour bench, a sun dial perhaps, a weather vane always seemed like an indulgence but I assumed a bird bath was a done deal. In my garden. The curse of bind weed.

Lucy   Seriously have we got weed?

Barbara   An abundance of bind weed and a plinth covered in bird shit.

She laughs, snorts as she laughs, starts to giggle at her loud snort, which sets **Lucy** *off and they're both crying with laughter. Silence.*

Lucy   I love you Mummy.

Barbara   I love you Lucy.

Lucy   I think we ought to perhaps talk before – I'm frightened. I –

Zac *enters, he's 30, tall, posh, off his head.*

Zac   Hi. Hi again.

Barbara   Would you like a cheese and jam sandwich as well Zac?

Zac *looks at* **Lucy** *and then back at* **Barbara** *and then back at Lucy again.*

Zac   Cheese and jam. That's. Unusual.

Lucy   And what?

Zac   But I can see how it might work. The cheesiness of the cheese and the jamminess of the jam.

Lucy   Listen you retard goon you're not judging the spastic special edition of *Masterchef*. Now get out your drugs and skin up.

Zac *laughs, thinks and then whispers something in* **Lucy**'s *ear.*

Barbara   What's that?

Lucy   He said 'I wouldn't venture into the WC'. How quaint. 'For half an hour'.

Zac *blushes bright red and* **Barbara** *laughs.*

Zac   That isn't right. Lucy that's just really cruel. Get out your own fucking drugs.

Lucy   Don't talk to me like that in front of my mother or I will cut off your balls and devil them like a pair of lamb's kidney's.

Barbara   Lucy I wish you would sometimes take your own advice and put on your chilling boots.

Zac *wants to laugh – doesn't.*

Lucy   I think I want to die.

Zac *laughs his head off.* **Barbara** *joins in, pleased to be the source of such hilarity.*

Lucy   Why are you laughing you don't even know what you're laughing at?

Silence.

I've been fired. From the show. I've been fired. I know I have.

Barbara   They've done what?

Lucy   My producer caught me. I was in my dressing room having a smoke. Only a tiny bit to chill me out. And. I don't know why. I, I hadn't locked my door and she knocked and came in with the script changes I told them to make. I freaked out. And she asked me to sit down and explain what I was doing when it was, you know, perfectly fucking obvious what I was doing. And she went mad. She was screaming and shouting at me and I calmed down a bit myself. And then she said she was going to speak to the Exec and I begged her not to. I begged her. And she told me she was going to get someone to come and baby-sit me. She actually said that, can you believe it? And she told me I had to say I wasn't feeling very well if anyone asked. And we wouldn't be filming the piece about the Shetland ponies. And I was so looking forward to it. They were going to film something else before they wasted any more time. And then just before she left she turned around and she said to me 'There are a million people waiting to take your place Lucy'. She actually said that! What a bitch.

Silence.

And then the Exec came down. Like the Headmaster. And he gave me an absolute bollocking. And it wasn't like he cared I was in bits or anything. And he was so angry about all the time and money that would be wasted because I would have to go home. And he said I had to understand how serious it was. Being caught doing something like that on a kids' show. And how the BBC couldn't have another scandal. They offered to ring someone and then they got me a car home. They've told me to say I've got gastric flu. But I think I am completely out. I can't even face talking to my agent. She's left me ten messages already and she's going nuts. I'm dead. I'm finished. That is it.

Barbara   For smoking a cigarette?

Lucy *explodes.*

Lucy   Are you a complete imbecile mother?

Silence.

Barbara   No.

Lucy *is about to cry – doesn't.*

Zac   It's wrong hey Barbara? Tiny little bit of brown. You'd think she'd had her face down in a pool of her own vomit.

Lucy   For God's sake shut up!

Barbara   How dare they?

Lucy   They can't do it to me can they?

Barbara   Well I won't let them.

Lucy   You can't stop it. I can't stop it. You can't stop it.

Barbara *goes to* **Lucy** *to try and comfort her but* **Lucy** *shrugs her off and walks away.*

Barbara   Darling we will get this all sorted out. Please don't worry.

Lucy   This is my life.

Silence.

Barbara   We will speak to your sister. Angela will write to them.

Lucy   No one knows. They're hushing it up. If they can. I don't think they can.

Barbara   Well they've no right.

Lucy *looks as if she will again explode.* **Barbara** *stops herself. Silence.*

Barbara   It will all blow over Lucy.

Lucy   It won't blow over. What am I going to do?

Silence.

Barbara   I knew all this was too good to be true.

She wipes away a tear. Silence.

Lucy   Pull yourself together mother please.

Zac   These people are tight man.

Lucy   Shut up Zac you couldn't hold down a job as a runner on Dave you useless cretin. This is all your fault.

Zac *looks at her.*

Lucy   You asked me if I wanted to try it. You did it.

Barbara   Did he?

Lucy   I was quite happy with my own class A drugs until that gangly twit hoved in to view.

Silence.

Barbara   How long has this been going on?

Lucy   We had some at a party last New Year's Eve.

Zac   It's cool Babs.

Barbara   Get out of this house now. I said now.

Silence.

Zac   No man she asked for it. And dat is the truth.

Lucy   What are you talking like that for? Wigger prick. He went to Harrow and he lives on Christchurch Hill with his mother and father.

Zac   You go too far Lucy.

Lucy   And what?

Zac   I'm gone. Don't call me. Because I will blank you and I will laugh at you when you're clucking.

Lucy   Fuck off.

Barbara   Yes. Please leave. Now.

Zac *nods at* **Barbara** *who points as if to indicate he should leave. He goes.*

Lucy   What am I going to do? I am utterly ruined. I don't think they can hush it up. I'm completely ruined Mummy. What am I going to do?

Silence.

Can I come and stay tonight?

Barbara   Darling of course.

Lucy   Just for tonight.

Barbara   You can come and stay with me. You can go in your old room. You'll be safe here. No one will harm you here.

Lucy   Won't they? I'm frightened it will all come out.

Barbara   You can stay here as long as you want.

Lucy   I don't know if I should.

Barbara   It's up to you darling. This is your home.

Silence.

Lucy   Can I? I would really appreciate it.

Barbara   You're here now and that's all that matters. You're going to let me look after you.

Lucy   Will you?

Barbara   Always.

Silence.

Lucy   Nothing is for always Mummy.

Barbara   Well I am. I want you to listen to me. Look at Mummy. I am here.

Silence.

And I will never let you down.

Two

*Lucy and her older sister **Angela**, thirty-six. **Angela** has just come into the kitchen at their mother's house. **Lucy** hasn't noticed. **Lucy** is rifling through **Angela**'s bag and finds her purse which she opens. **Lucy** notices **Angela** staring at her and drops it.*

Angela   What are you doing with my purse?

Silence.

Angela   You had it there in your hand.

Lucy *thinks.*

Lucy   I didn't.

Angela   I saw it.

Lucy   It's on the floor.

Angela   Because you dropped it on the floor.

Lucy   Are you mad Angela?

Angela   I saw you drop it on the floor.

Lucy   Are you mad?

Angela   I came in and saw you drop it on the floor.

Lucy   No you didn't. I'm making a cup of tea, would you like one?

Angela   I saw you drop it.

Lucy   No I'm sorry Angela you didn't.

Angela   I saw you.

Lucy   Have you got a cigarette?

Angela   I saw you do it.

Lucy   Cigarette?

Angela   I saw you.

Silence.

Why are you lying to me?

Lucy   I asked you for a cigarette.

Angela   Why are you lying to me?

Lucy   Have you got a cigarette?

Angela   Why are you telling me a bare-faced lie when you know perfectly well what happened was that I came in here to the kitchen to fetch my handbag, I saw you with my purse and you dropped it on the floor?

Lucy   You're not in Highbury Corner Magistrates' Court now.

Angela   You're telling a bare-faced lie. I saw you.

Lucy   Sorry Angela you didn't.

Angela   I saw.

Lucy   So steely. You really should have taken silk. You would have gone far.

Angela   You mean like you?

Silence.

Lucy   Really this is so boring.

Angela   I know what you are.

Silence.

We both know.

Lucy   Have you got a cigarette or not?

Angela   So why lie about something we both know has happened?

Lucy   Are you deaf as well as crazy?

Angela   We both know the truth of what's going on here.

Lucy   Go away Angela.

Angela   So why did you tell me a bare-faced lie?

Lucy   You're not in charge any more.

Angela   Why do you continue to tell me these bare-faced lies?

Lucy   You're the liar.

Angela   My eyes did not lie.

Lucy   Are you on drugs?

Angela   And my breaking heart is not lying to me either.

Silence.

Lucy   Mum, Angela's off of her tits!

Angela   When are you going to leave?

Silence.

Lucy   When you get out of my face.

Angela   I mean really it's silly your flat sitting empty.

Lucy   Mum's lonely.

Silence.

Angela   She's been doing perfectly well for the last six years.

Lucy   Oh yeah forgot she doesn't confide in you, because you have no time to listen to her.

Silence.

Angela   When are you going home?

Lucy   I can't.

Angela   There's no such thing as can't.

Lucy   Someone else is there.

Angela   Well throw them out.

Lucy   I need the money.

Angela   Evidently.

Silence.

This is absurd. Wake up Lucy.

Lucy   Can't help you there sister.

Angela   Wake up.

Lucy   I am awake.

Angela   You know that's not what I mean.

Lucy   I'm awake! I'm alive! Look! I'm alive you deaf cunt!

Silence.

Angela   Why are you doing this to me?

Lucy   Oh have I upset you sister?

Angela   Angela will do.

Lucy   Have I sister?

Angela   My name is Angela thank you very much.

Silence.

Lucy   Have I upset you sister?

Angela   I told you Angela will do.

Lucy   I know Angela will do, Angela, but you're my beloved sister, sister.

Angela   What are you doing with the rent from your flat?

Lucy   I don't know.

Angela   Does Mum know what you're doing with the money?

Lucy   It's my money.

Angela   But as I understand it mother dear has one hundred thousand pounds equity in your flat. And if it is worth four hundred thousand pounds, say, then she is entitled if not to 25 per cent of the monies, 25 per cent of the say.

Lucy   Please, Angela when you leave this house grab hold of the first man you see and let him fuck you.

Angela   Does she know?

Lucy   Ask her yourself.

Angela   Oh I will.

Lucy   You've lost it. You've gone and lost the plot at last! I always knew you would! Mum Angela's on drugs!

Angela   And who exactly is living in your flat?

Lucy   I don't know, ask mother. If she can remember. Have you got that cigarette or not?

Angela *takes a packet of cigarettes from her own pocket. She shows* **Lucy** *she has one left and then puts it in her own mouth and lights it. Silence.*

Lucy *very calmly removes it from* **Angela***'s lips and smokes it herself.*

Lucy   You know its been a complete disappointment to me that my beloved older sister has always finally behaved in such a childish way.

Silence.

Look I was only checking to see if Mummy had taken any money from your purse. She hides my money all the time. As if I'm a child. And she tries to steal my Visa card as well!

Silence.

She's always saying to me she hasn't got any money when I need something.

Silence.

Angela   Really? I wonder why. Why do you think she's hiding your money Lucy?

Lucy   I don't believe her do you?

Angela   I don't anything any more Lucylu.

Silence.

Lucy   She's lying.

Angela   What have I ever done to you?

Lucy   Mummy's a freak. She is a freak.

Angela   What have I ever done to you? What could I have ever done, would you tell me please Lucy?

Barbara *enters with a glass of red wine in her hand.*

Barbara   Was someone calling?

Angela   Did you know Lucy has let off her flat?

Barbara   Ash tray Lucy dear.

Angela   Did you know?

Barbara   Yes darling. I let it off for her.

Angela   And where is that money going?

Barbara   When the letting agent has taken his share and Lucy's accountant has kept a portion towards your sister's tax bill I suppose the rest plops into her bank account.

Angela   And what do you think she is doing with that money?

Barbara   I expect she's spending it.

Angela   I see.

Barbara   She is a grown woman.

Angela   Then what is she doing here?

Barbara   It won't be long before she's feeling better and gets back to work and popping here there and everywhere like she used to. She is ill. Angela why are you always bossing me around and telling me what to do?

Silence.

Angela   And what about the hundred thousand pounds she owes you?

Barbara   She will repay the money when the flat is sold. Whenever that is. Ashtray Lucy.

Angela   And you believe that is what will happen now do you?

Barbara   Yes I do.

Angela   The way things are turning out.

Barbara   Lucy has given her word.

Angela   Well quite frankly –

Barbara   Why am I always treated like a child by you Angela?

Angela   I wonder. Is that the second glass or the second bottle?

Silence.

Barbara   'What is a cynic? A man who knows the price of everything and the value of nothing.'

Angela   Bravo Mother. If only your book of quotations held me in the same thrall it did when I was doing my A-levels. Why do you prefer her to me?

Barbara   There's never been any favouritism.

Lucy   Give me a cuddle Angela.

Angela *smiles and removes the wine glass from* **Barbara** *and drinks.* **Barbara** *calmly removes it from her daughter's hand and drinks herself.* **Lucy** *watches eagerly.*

Angela   Why do you prefer her to me?

Barbara   I don't.

Angela   Why do you prefer her to me?

Barbara   I don't.

Angela   Why do you prefer her to me?

Barbara   I said I don't.

Angela   Why do you prefer her to me?

Barbara   Angela.

Angela   Why do you prefer her to me?

Barbara   Angela dear.

Angela   Why do you prefer her to me?

Barbara   You're so boring when you're like this Angela. I do wish you would go home.

Silence.

Lucy   No stay Angela.

Angela   Why?

Barbara   Because Lucy is nice to me. Lucy doesn't talk at me.

Angela   When she wants something.

Barbara   If only you could see how you are towards me. This isn't about you Angela.

Angela   And it never is, is it? I have never asked you for a penny.

Barbara   Perhaps you wish you had?

Angela   Perhaps I do. You would have had to consider my needs

Silence.

Barbara   How much would you like?

Angela   That's not the point.

Barbara   But I thought it was your point exactly? Perhaps you would like your half now? I'm sure looking into the coldness in your eyes, you wish me dead anyway.

Silence.

Angela   I don't need your money.

Barbara   But it's not about what you need, it's about what you want and what you wish you had. Why, when you've had all of life's advantages, are you so full of anger?

Angela   I actually feel incredibly calm now.

Barbara   You only have to accept that you're a tough and Lucy is delicate. You are different and you always have been.

Angela   Well how wrong you are.

Silence.

If she were mine and she were under my roof I'd make her wash. She smells. I'd make her wash her mouth out and hair out with soap. I'd make her scrub her own dirty knickers and scrub and scrub her teeth with her toothbrush until her gums –

Barbara   Well what a cruel mother you will make. If you ever find a man that will have you.

Silence.

Angela   It seems to me as someone who spends her whole life trying to establish the facts in one miserable story or other, that what is happening to her and what she is doing to you is quite self-evident.

Barbara   They are your facts not mine.

Angela   As they always have been. And that is why this family is screwed.

Silence.

Barbara   You pain me.

Angela   What hackneyed neatness. One daughter who battles with reality and another who flees from it.

Silence.

Barbara   I must say I am hurt.

Angela   I intended to hurt you. As you did me.

Silence.

Barbara   I never would have expected such an adolescent argument with a woman of thirty-six years of age.

Angela   I won't come back.

Barbara   Then that is your decision.

Angela   I won't.

Barbara   Don't threaten me.

Angela   I assure you it's not a threat.

Barbara   Then you had better leave.

Lucy   Don't go Angela, it's boring when you're not here.

Angela *looks at* **Lucy** *for a very long time.*

Barbara   Goodbye Angela.

Angela   Goodbye Lucy. Goodbye Mum.

She goes. Silence.

Lucy   Where's she gone?

Barbara   Home. To her house.

Three

Lucy *is lying on the floor resting her head on a smart cushion.*

She has a pint glass full of liquid which looks like apple or orange juice nearby. There's something else lying by too.

Barbara *comes in. She has two Waitrose shopping bags full of groceries. She looks at* **Lucy**.

Barbara Lucy darling why don't you lie on the sofa. It will be much more comfortable. I'll fetch a blanket.

She spots something which stops her in her tracks. She puts down the groceries and goes to where **Lucy** *is lying. As she kneels down to pick up the thing she has seen she absentmindedly knocks over the pint of liquid.*

Barbara Oh no.

She picks up the object which has attracted her attention. It's a hypodermic needle and syringe. **Lucy** *has been shooting up.* **Barbara** *screams.* **Lucy** *begins to come round.* **Barbara** *begins to shake her and freak out.*

Barbara What have you done Lucy? What have you done? Lucy? Lucy!

Lucy Take your hands off of me. Now!

Barbara You promised me.

Lucy Don't yell.

Barbara Lucy!

Lucy Zac's dead.

Barbara My God. Lucy.

Silence.

Who is dead?

Lucy My friend.

Barbara I don't know who you mean darling. Who is dead?

Lucy   Zac.

Barbara   Zac?

Lucy   Yes.

Barbara   Lucy have you been out?

Lucy   I was upset.

Barbara   What have you been doing Lucy?

Lucy   I was upset Mummy.

Barbara   You promised me you would never do this.

Lucy   I'm sorry.

Barbara   You promised me faithfully and I believed you.

Lucy   I'm sorry I'm bad.

Barbara   Lucy there's blood! What have you done?

Lucy   It was a bit of an effort trying to do it on my own.

Barbara *fights back tears. Wipes them away and then inadvertently puts her hand in the spilt liquid. Something isn't right.* **Barbara** *smells her hand.*

Barbara   Darling what is this?

Lucy   I needed a wee.

Silence.

Barbara   You?

Lucy   I needed a wee.

Silence.

Barbara   Okay.

Lucy   I was upset.

Barbara   I know darling.

Lucy   Zac was my friend.

Barbara   I know.

Lucy   He understood me.

Barbara   I know he did.

Lucy   He was my friend.

Barbara   I know.

Lucy   I had to go out.

Barbara   Darling where did you get the money?

Lucy   I couldn't find where you'd put my debit card and my credit card.

Barbara   Lucy, I had to cut them up. There are new ones coming. You don't need any money darling.

Lucy's *face contorts and then relaxes. Contorts and then relaxes.*

Lucy   I do. I had to go out.

Barbara   Lucy what happened?

Lucy   I met a man in Clissold Park.

Lucy's *face contorts and then relaxes.*

Barbara   What did he do Lucy?

Lucy   You know what he did Mummy.

This is too much for **Barbara** *to hear. She turns away from* **Lucy** *full of her own inner agony. Silence.*

Barbara *steels herself and goes to the groceries. She takes out some multi-surface cleaner and angrily pulls a spanking new tea towel from its cardboard packaging. She looks at* **Lucy**.

Lucy   I'm sorry.

Barbara   I know darling.

She goes to **Lucy**, *and then gets down on her hands and knees and begins cleaning up the spilt piss. She takes her time, as long as it takes. All her anguish, pain and hurt is somehow manifest in the cleaning up of* **Lucy**'s *piss. Silence.*

Barbara   You mustn't go out Lucy.

Lucy   I know.

Barbara   You will get into trouble.

Lucy   I'm sorry.

Barbara   People will find out. People will find out the truth. And they mustn't.

Lucy   I think they will.

Barbara   It will make it harder.

Lucy   I know.

Barbara   It will only make it harder for you to go back to work when you're feeling better.

Lucy*'s face contorts and then relaxes.*

Barbara   So you have to do what Mummy says.

Lucy   I'm sorry Mummy.

Barbara   What happened to Zac?

Lucy*'s face contorts and then relaxes.*

Barbara   You don't have to tell me if you don't want to. You can tell me later. When you're feeling better.

Lucy   He died in the hospital.

Barbara   Did he?

Lucy   The lady at the hospital rang me up.

Barbara   Did she?

Lucy   Yes she did.

Barbara   What did she say?

Lucy   She said my phone number was on a piece of paper in his Oyster card.

Barbara   And how did he die?

Lucy   You know how he died Mummy.

Lucy's *face contorts and then relaxes. Silence.*

Barbara *finishes cleaning up. She puts the tea towel in the pint glass. She comes over and sits by* **Lucy**'s *feet.* **Barbara** *tries to take* **Lucy**'s *foot in her hands so she can rub it. But* **Lucy** *doesn't like her feet being touched and moves her foot.* **Barbara** *tries again and* **Lucy** *moves her foot.* **Barbara** *tries again and* **Lucy** *gives in.* **Barbara** *massages* **Lucy**'s *foot.*

Barbara   There was a drunk in Waitrose. A black man. Must have been six foot tall. No shoes and a long green coat, which looked like it must have been something. You know before. The pockets were torn. He fell into a little Jewish lady. And she dropped all her groceries. I picked up the dates. The asparagus. And we watched the security guards and the policemen pull him away. He was screaming. Almost hysterically Lucy. Foaming and drooling. I was formulating my anger into something pithy. To raise a smile. But little old lady looked at me. And I caught a whiff of something. Of her judging me. Intuitively judging me Lucylu. And she said, 'There but for the Grace of God go you and I'. Smiled. Nodded rather formally actually, and turned away. And picked up a packet of Quinoa. Which she can't have had any intention of buying. John Bradford said it I think. 'There but for the Grace of God goes John Bradford.' He was burned at the stake at Newgate prison. I shall have to check my book or it will annoy me.

Silence.

I walked along Holloway Road in a blind fury. And must have let half a dozen taxis go by before I focused on flagging one down. How dare that little Jewess judge me like that? That vagrant had nothing to do with me. He has nothing to do with my life.

Silence.

And me in Waitrose and you in Clissold Park.

Silence.

Lucy   You need to give me money.

Barbara   I know but darling –

Lucy   It's no use trying to pull wool over my eyes.

Barbara   I know darling but –

Lucy   You don't know what it's like.

Silence

Barbara   I'm only trying to do my best.

Silence

Give me a cuddle Lucy.

Lucy *sits right up. Allows* **Barbara** *to hold her.*

Lucy   When I ask for money you have to give me money otherwise. Otherwise. There are all manner of terrible things which can happen. Zac would never let me inject. He'd never let – he was so selfish. Fellow travellers. Smokers of opium. Yeah right. You know if you're going to do it, let's fucking do it. Bring it on. I'm glad the twit died. Injecting without telling me. Liar.

Her face contorts and then relaxes.

Barbara   What's it like?

Lucy   What?

Barbara   I need to know. I need to know. I can't – Why – I, I need to know.

Silence.

Lucy   Imagine me inside your tummy again. It's lovely. The best cuddle of your life. Calm. Calmness. A snoring dog in a new basket. Lovely. Under the blanket. Like when I was small.

Silence.

I've needed something. For such a long time. And I never knew what it was. Until today. I never once Mummy.

Silence.

Barbara   Go on.

Silence.

Lucy   Everything else is background now. Tap and modern and ballet, horse-riding and learning to play the flute. Theatre school and singing lessons and learning to inhale cigarettes and being fingered by boys with Coca-Cola breath. And auditions and making tea and skits on the radio and producers with wandering hands and wives. And being constantly perky and sunny and cheeky and charming and blonde and rosy and game. Constantly game. Let's fucking send a wrecking ball through that one. Hey Mummy. Everyone knows that people in terrible kids' TV are the worst. Let's cane it. Let's smoke it. Let's chop it up and snort it. Cut it. Pass it on and skank the clueless. Baking powder will do. And be ready to let a snail crawl up your arm at nine in the morning with a bastard behind the eyes. Be prepared. And now I'm at my mother's house.

Her face contorts and then relaxes.

Lucy   I was almost famous. I almost made it.

Silence.

Not any more Mummy. Everything is background. I know what completeness is. I have seen the face of God. Speedball.

Silence.

Barbara   You must tell me how much you want. You must tell me when you need it. I will give you the money. Please promise me you won't go to Clissold Park again. Promise me.

Lucy   On my life.

Silence.

That's all I wanted.

Silence.

Did I tell you?

Barbara   Tell me what darling?

Lucy   My friend.

Barbara   Yes?

Lucy   Zac. Zac is dead.

Four

The accident and emergency department of the Whittington Hospital. Early hours of the morning.

Lucy *is on a hospital trolley. A man, Pete, towers over her. With some cheap flowers.*

Pete   Really it was quite easy to come in.

Lucy   I'm sure.

Pete   It was.

Lucy   Obviously.

Pete   Never been easier.

Lucy   I'll come and find you later.

Pete   But we need to sort things out.

Lucy   Well how can I sort things out now?

Pete   That's not my problem.

Lucy   Okay Pete.

Pete   I think the security man is new.

Lucy   Whatever.

Pete   And I think these helped.

Pete *puts the flowers down on the trolley. Silence.*

Lucy   So what do you expect me to do?

Pete   You look better.

Lucy   I haven't got anything on me at all.

Pete   I thought you were dead.

Lucy   I don't know what's happened to my bag or my purse.

Pete   Have they given you an injection?

Lucy   Yes in my bottom and it really fucking hurt.

Pete   Was it Naloxone?

Lucy   I don't know.

Pete   I thought you were gone.

Lucy   Then why didn't you ring an ambulance?

Pete   Why don't I believe you when you say you don't have nothing on you? I think you skanked me Lucy.

Lucy   Well if you hadn't fucking run off and left me to die then you would know where you were wouldn't you?

Pete   There were two more wraps.

Lucy   Fuck off.

Pete   I went back there.

Lucy   Just fuck off before I start to scream.

Pete *produces a Stanley knife from his left pocket which he gestures with.*

Pete   I went back and there weren't no signs of nothing there.

Lucy   Fuck off.

Pete   The posh girl always got something. Dat much I know.

He slips his right hand under the cover of the sheet towards **Lucy**'*s groin.*

Lucy   Move your hand now or I will scream this whole fucker down.

Pete *ignores her and feels to see if she has hidden a wrap of heroin in her vagina.*

Pete   If you think I will hesitate in cutting your face in half then you must think again.

Satisfied nothing is there he removes his hand from under the covers. He smiles. Sniffs the scent on his fingers.

Pete   It's a long time since I sampled that sweet smell of pussy.

Lucy   How dare you.

Pete I must say I never thought of you dat way.

Lucy How dare you.

Pete But maybe we should get to know each other in a new way.

Lucy I'd rather fuck a rabid dog then let you anywhere near me you disgusting beast.

Silence.

Pete Now two, is forty you owe me. Forty notes. Forty on the nose.

Lucy I don't know what happened to your gear. I was unconscious at the time.

Pete You see I have always had a rule which has served me well. Never believe a junkie.

Lucy How dare you call me a junkie.

Pete You got it, I know you have.

Lucy This is ridiculous. All that's happened is I OD'd and you ran away and left me to die on my own and somewhere and at some point you lost your gear.

Pete Don't start back-chatting me.

Lucy And then you started to feel guilty about what you did.

Pete I ain't got nothing to feel bad about!

Lucy You started to feel guilty and you started to cluck.

Pete Shut up now!

Lucy And you didn't have your gear and you wanted someone to blame.

Pete *threatens her with the knife.*

Pete Did you put it in your batty?

Lucy What?

Pete   Did you hide my gear in your bottom? You heard me.

Lucy   No Pete I didn't.

Pete   Roll over.

Lucy   No.

Pete   I said roll over.

Barbara *enters. She has a handbag over one arm.* **Pete** *puts the knife back in his pocket so* **Barbara** *doesn't see it.*

Barbara   Hello.

Lucy   This is my friend Pete. I was telling him how they pronounced me dead. And then I came back. But he's going now.

Barbara   Thank you for coming to visit.

Pete   No problem.

Barbara   Bless you, Lucy hasn't got many friends.

Pete   I know.

Lucy   Mummy before he goes could you give him the forty pounds he says I owe him.

Silence

Barbara   Was it you?

Pete   What?

Barbara   Was it you that gave it to her?

Pete   No.

Lucy   Just give him the money and he'll go away.

Barbara *thinks and then puts her handbag on the bed. She takes out her purse and two twenty-pound notes. She goes to* **Pete** *and gives him the money.*

Pete   Good.

Barbara *slaps him as hard as she can around the face. Silence.*

Pete   You can have that one for free. But you touch me again and I will shank you.

Pete *brings out the Stanley knife.*

Barbara   Please do your worst. You will go to prison and never be able to come near my daughter again. Go on. Please.

Silence.

Pete   You are Wacko Jacko.

Barbara   She was pronounced dead! I lost my husband when she was only a baby and I won't lose Lucy before her time! Get out!

Pete   You're freaking me out woman. I want more money. Now!

Barbara   Go away. Go on. Go away. Get out.

Lucy   Do what my mother says or I will scream.

Pete *thinks and puts away the Stanley knife and makes to go.*

Pete   Your daughter's a whore who takes it up the Gary for smack you old dried up bitch. I hope you die of cancer.

He goes. **Lucy** *closes her eyes. Her face contorts. Silence.*

Barbara *makes to go to* **Lucy**.

Lucy   No.

Barbara *returns to her bag. She takes a little hip flask out and has a quick nip of brandy.*

Lucy   Can I have some?

Silence.

Barbara   No Lucy.

She returns the hip flask to her bag and looks at **Lucy**. *She goes to* **Lucy** *and gets on the bed with her. She holds* **Lucy** *and they hold each other for a long time.*

Lucy   Are you okay?

Barbara   Yes. Are you?

Lucy   Yes I think so. I love you Mummy.

Barbara   I love you Lucy.

Five

Barbara's large house in Islington, a few weeks later.

Angela and Barbara talk. The cordless house phone sits between them. Barbara drinks red wine.

Angela   I'm pleased you called.

Barbara   It's been hard.

Angela   Yes it has been hard.

Barbara   Yes.

Angela   How are you?

Barbara   Not good.

Angela   Well I'm here now.

Barbara   Yes you arc darling.

Angela   I am pleased you called me.

Barbara   Well yes.

Angela   I can't think of the last time you asked me to come.

Barbara   Well then we're both pleased.

Angela   Even before.

Barbara   Before?

Angela   Mother it's been a year.

Silence

Barbara   It hasn't?

Angela   It has.

Barbara   Well I can't believe it's been a year.

Angela   I thought we really had fallen out this time.

Barbara   Well how could you think that?

Angela   I'm ashamed to admit it, but this time I couldn't pick up the phone.

Barbara   Why are you compelled to go over things?

Angela   But you did. I never thought you would but you did.

Barbara   Yes I did.

Angela   You phoned, you called me.

Barbara   Darling I am your mother and you are my daughter.

Silence

Angela   Yes, I know.

Barbara   Let's not pick over the bones.

Angela   Okay, okay.

Barbara   Good.

Angela   Do you have any idea what a hard time I've had?

Barbara   No.

Angela   I met someone.

Barbara   Oh good.

Angela   And he left me. About two months ago.

Barbara   Well I've rather put my foot in it.

Angela   I can't tell you how it's made me feel about myself.

Barbara   Well you will soon find another.

Angela   Mummy I had an ectopic pregnancy.

She fights back tears. She won't cry in front of her mother. Silence.

Barbara   I wish I had known.

Angela   I'm sorry.

Barbara   I would have liked to have been able to support you.

Angela   I love you Mummy.

Barbara   I love you Angela. I regret very much the ugly things I said the last time we spoke. I've hated us falling out. Lucy's easy. She likes simple things. I don't always understand you Angela. I can't help it. I am so sorry.

Angela *walks into her mother's arms and they embrace for some time.*

Barbara   Do you know why I called you Angela? Do you remember?

Angela   Of course I do.

Barbara   Because you looked like an angel on my bosom.

Angela *detaches herself from* **Barbara** *and walks away with her arms folded.*

Angela   Where's Lucy?

Silence.

Barbara   She's not here.

Angela   Has she gone out?

Barbara   I don't know where she is.

Angela   I see.

Barbara   I've been in a frightful state.

Angela   Right.

Barbara   I daren't take my eyes off of the phone.

Angela   Oh yes there it is.

Barbara   In the last few months she's been inclined to wander off.

Angela   Right.

Barbara   But she always turns up. Like a bad penny.

Angela   I'm sure you don't mean that.

Barbara   Would you like a glass of wine?

Angela   No.

Silence.

How long has she been gone this time?

Barbara   A fortnight.

Silence.

I'm having all the red tops delivered and I can't sleep because I'm convinced she's going to turn up on the front of the paper in a gutter and it will come out and her life will be ruined.

Angela   I wouldn't worry about the tabloid press. They don't even know who she is and insofar as I'm aware she's never slept with a footballer.

Barbara   Please don't take that tone.

Silence.

Angela   If you hadn't rather over-egged the pudding with 'an angel on my bosom' I might not have grasped so quickly how shallow your motive in contacting me was.

Barbara   No.

Angela   Still none of us ever has done subtlety well. I don't know why the working class get such a bad press. I find the middle class infinitely crasser.

Barbara   I think you're being dreadfully unfair.

Angela   Am I?

Barbara   All I've been thinking is how have I managed to lose both of my daughters.

Silence.

Angela   You haven't lost us.

Barbara   Haven't I?

Angela   Lucy will turn up.

Barbara   And you?

Silence.

Well your silence gives me the answer.

Angela   There's no such thing as unconditional love Mother.

Barbara   Well you will know better if you ever have children. Ignore me. I'm sorry. I can't –

Angela   What? Help yourself?

Barbara   No.

Silence.

I will always love my daughters.

Angela   Why do you love me?

Barbara   I am your mother.

Angela   Yes but how do you love me?

Barbara   Well I love you.

Angela   Yes but what is it about me? Me.

Barbara   Angela you're so wilful, how can one describe all the emotions in the world?

Angela   I'm not asking for them all.

Barbara   Really you're like a terrier with a bone.

Angela   I'm not asking for all the reasons I'm only asking for one. What is one thing that you love about me?

Barbara   Why do you always require a reason?

Angela   Because it's the way I am.

Barbara   Really.

Angela   And because I would like to hear something apart from the fact I am obviously cynical, wilful, I'm hard-nosed, a tough, a cold woman with men and a bit frumpy.

Barbara   I won't argue with you now. Take off your coat and I'll fetch you a glass of wine.

Angela   I don't want a glass of wine.

Silence.

Why is it you have never been able to love me?

Barbara   I have done my best.

Angela   You're not even engaged with reality. For God's sake you can't even accept the truth of how Daddy died!

Silence.

It might have been easy to pull the wool over the eyes of a little nine-year-old girl but I am a grown woman now.

At that precise moment the phone begins to ring. **Barbara** *snatches it up. She goes white as she listens to the voice on the other end.*

Barbara   Calm down Lucy I can't hear you. Darling calm down.

The phone line evidently goes dead.

Barbara   Lucy! Lucy! Lucy darling I'm here I'm coming to fetch you! Lucy!

Barbara *is helpless and doesn't know what to do. She gulps down the wine she has left. She looks at the empty wine glass and the phone receiver. Silence.*

Angela   What's happened?

Barbara   She said she needs some money her dealer's going to kill her. Then she screamed and the line went dead. It went dead.

Barbara *collapses, not physically, but internally, a sort of internal collapse leaving her whimpering like a dying animal.* **Angela** *takes the glass and phone off her on reflex.*

Angela   Where is she?

Barbara   I don't know.

Angela   The police will be no use unless we know where she is.

Barbara   She didn't say she was frightened and she was screaming.

Angela   I don't know what I can do.

Silence.

Barbara   She's going to end up dead isn't she?

Angela   No Mum.

Barbara   If not tonight another night.

Silence.

My Lucy dead. No, no, no, never, never, never. Pull yourself together.

She stifles a sob and slaps her own face.

Angela   No.

Barbara   We've got to do something. Tell me what to do Angela. You were always the sensible one.

Angela   I don't know what to do.

Barbara   I know you hate me but I am begging you to tell me what to do.

Angela   I don't hate you Mummy.

Barbara *gets down on her knees to plead.*

Barbara   I know you hate me. I'm sorry I'm such a hopeless mother but you must help me with Lucy.

She begins to repeatedly slap herself about her cheeks.

Angela   Mum please.

Barbara   I can't. You see I've run out. It's no wonder you hate me.

Angela   There's nothing we can do.

Barbara   There must be.

Angela   What can we do?

Barbara   There must be something we can do.

Angela   There's nothing we can do.

Barbara   But there must be.

Angela   Only Lucy can help herself now.

Barbara   No.

Angela   It's the truth.

Barbara   No, I must be able to help my girl in some way.

Angela   You know in your heart in your bones you've done everything you can for her.

Barbara   No.

Angela   Well I don't know what I can do.

Barbara   There must be something more I can do.

Angela   She's better off on her own, you're only enabling her habit.

Barbara *explodes.*

Barbara   I am helping her! I am protecting her!

Silence.

Why has this happened to us? Things like this don't happen to families like ours! Why? Tell me Angela why?

Angela   I don't know Mum. I think I should go. It was a mistake to come. It was silly of me to think things could be any different.

Silence.

Barbara   Please don't leave me on my own tonight Angela.

Silence.

Angela.

Angela   Mum you can't expect me to drop everything. I –
God this is awful.

Barbara   Angela darling.

Angela   Oh God.

Barbara   Angela darling.

Angela   Mum stop, get up.

Barbara   Angela.

Angela *takes a deep breath and looks at her mother. She passes*
Barbara *the wine glass and phone back. And then takes off her coat*
which she puts over one arm. She helps her mother up.

Barbara   Thank you darling. Bless you.

Angela   Under the circumstances how could I possibly do
anything else?

Six

The accident and emergency department of the Whittington Hospital. Early hours of the morning.

Lucy *is sitting up on a hospital trolley. She is a complete state, a transformation from the person we met at the beginning of the play. She has a bad cut on her right hand which she holds aloft and the blood runs down her forearm. A nurse,* **Brian**, *comes in and attends to her.*

Lucy Chop, chop.

Brian Very funny.

Lucy Chop, chop I say my dear man.

Brian Right Lucy I'm going to need to clean that up.

Lucy Well be sharp about it.

Brian No one told me we had Lady Muck in tonight. It's not what it says on your notes pet.

Lucy Fucking pet fucking cunt fucking cheeky cunt.

Brian Okay darling this is how it is. You either cut out the abusive language or I fetch the security man and you're out of here do you understand me?

Lucy *looks at him and smiles very sweetly.*

Lucy I'm sorry nurse. My hand hurts.

Brian Okay.

Brian *goes to work cleaning up* **Lucy**'s *hand before he stitches it.*

Lucy Please be careful I need to look after my hand.

Brian Don't worry.

Lucy Thank you Mr Nurse.

Brian So how did you cut your hand?

Lucy I don't know.

Brian   I think someone said you had a fight.

Lucy   Well that's a lie.

Brian   So how did you do it?

Lucy   I must have fallen over.

Brian   Where did you fall over then?

Lucy   I can't remember.

Brian   Right.

Lucy   Do you know who I am?

Brian   No pet but I'm sure you're going to tell me.

Lucy   I am not exactly at liberty to say exactly but when you find out about my television pedigree you'll regret treating me like dirt.

Brian *takes a step back from her and takes a good look at her.*

Brian   Well I can't say I recognise you.

Lucy   I've been poorly and taken some time off that's why.

Brian   Is it you and that Amy Winehouse?

Lucy   I don't think you would know my work as you don't look like the sort of person who might have children.

Brian *laughs and shakes his head.*

Brian   Right we're going to put a stitch or two in and you can get off home. Wherever that is.

Lucy   Do I have to go tonight?

Brian   Yes pet you do.

Lucy   Please don't.

Brian   Where do you live?

Silence.

Right let's get this done.

He gives **Lucy** *a local anesthetic.*

Brian   I once met a doctor who liked a bit of smack on the side. He said he found shooting up very erotic. The injection of liquid in to a body. Pulling back and the blood. Can't see it myself. My God he was a big man.

He begins to stitch up **Lucy**'s *hand. It still hurts a touch.*

Brian   You know I stitched up a chap last week who claimed to be the grandson of Hermann Göring. Claimed his grandmother was some sort of servant at Berchtesgaden and she had a bit of a –

He whistles.

With the fat Nazi just before the end of the war. Quite convincing he were. Went on and on about how he'd tried to contact his aunt who was Göring's only daughter or summat. Reckoned he'd been to Munich and South Africa in search of her. He liked a bit of smack as well this homeless chap did. Told me he'd taken it up so he could commune with his grandfather who'd been addicted himself. Shot in the groin he was in the beer hall putsch. Had too much morphine for his pain. Same thing with one of our other regulars. Ex-Russian soldier wounded in Chechnia. Homeless as well. Same thing. Memory of an elephant I've got. Never forget a face. Never forget a fact. Available for pub quizzes on Tuesdays and Thursdays. Of course the grandson of Hermann Göring was all fabrication and I tried to humour him but you mustn't go along with a delusion really.

Lucy   I know what you're trying to do and I'm afraid you don't know what you're talking about.

Brian   So if you're a TV presenter how come you're sleeping rough?

The local anaesthetic is wearing off and **Lucy** *yelps with pain as* **Brian** *finishes up.*

Brian   I'm sorry did I catch you?

He catches her good hand very gently in a gesture of kindness. He lets go.

Lucy   I'm not sleeping rough I'm staying with friends.

Brian   Fine okay fine whatever you say there's no flies on me.

Lucy   I'm staying with friends okay.

Brian   Okay.

Lucy   I'm staying with friends. I've millions of friends. Millions of them. More than you will ever have.

Brian   What is it love?

He looks at her. **Lucy** *takes his hand and then withdraws it after a few moments.*

Brian   Lucy?

Lucy *offers her hand back.* **Brian** *is wary of taking it.*

Brian   Lucy? What happened to you pet?

Lucy *shakes her head.*

Brian   Can you not go home? Have you had a falling out at home?

Lucy   No.

Brian   Why don't you go back then?

Lucy's *face contorts and then relaxes.*

Lucy   Please hold my hand.

Brian *holds her good hand uneasily.*

Brian   Go on love spit it out.

Lucy   I am going to be famous. I am.

Brian   What is it?

Lucy   I was on the television. I was.

Brian   Lucy.

Lucy   It was on CBBC and it was called the *Animal House* and everyone said it was going to be a winner and I've seen that bitch they've put on there instead of me and she's not a patch on me.

Her face contorts and then relaxes.

Brian   Did someone attack you?

Lucy   I love the animals.

Brian   Does someone want to harm you?

Lucy   I love them. The birds, the bees, the snails. I love them. You're a kind man.

Brian   It's my job to be kind.

Lucy *looks at him. Silence.*

Lucy   I think I'm in a bit of a spot.

Brian   Go on.

Lucy   I think I'm in a bit of a pickle.

Brian   Go, go for it, go on I'm listening. I'm here.

Lucy *grips* **Brian***'s hand and whispers in his ear. He looks at her. She nods.*

Brian   I'm sorry.

Lucy *begins to cry but holds herself in. She thinks. Jumps off of the bed.*

Lucy   I'm going. I've had enough of this.

Brian   No don't – let me make a phone call first.

Lucy   You can't keep me here!

She begins to rage.

Lucy   Do you think you can lock me up like my mother? Do you? Do you? Do you? Well you can't!

Brian   I've a phone number I can ring if you will just –

Lucy   Just what?

Brian   Just stop for a moment pet and think about what you just whispered in my ear. I'd like to help you.

Lucy   I don't need your fucking help! I don't need anyone! I'm fine! I'm fine! Fuck off with your help!

Silence.

Brian *changes his posture as if to show she is free to leave.* **Lucy** *panics.*

Lucy   Please help me, please help me I've ruined my life, what have I done, what have I done? Please help me.

Brian *goes to her and comforts her.*

Lucy   Help me, I need help. I can't stand it any more. I want to die. I'd rather die than be locked in this circle of hell any more. I can't do it I can't do it.

Brian   I know, I know.

Lucy   Help me Mr Nurse.

Brian   There, there.

At this phrase **Lucy** *pulls away from* **Brian**.

Brian   Lucy what is it?

Lucy *shakes her head. Silence.*

Brian   Will you be okay for a minute while I pop out and call someone down to see you?

Lucy   No.

Brian   I need to pop out.

Lucy   You said you would help me?

Brian   And I will.

Lucy   Please help me.

Brian   I will.

Lucy   Help me.

Brian   I will I promise you I'll get someone down and when they've examined you I'm going to give you a number you can ring and they'll do what they can.

Lucy   It's not the police is it, I can't have any scandals.

Brian   No.

Lucy   Help me Mr Nurse.

Brian   Lucy you told me you've been raped.

Lucy *nods. Silence.*

She has a full-on panic attack. She tries to breathe and then begins to get control of herself.

Brian   Easy. Good girl. That's it deep breaths. Deep breaths. Now Lucy pet you're not going to disappear on me are you when I pop out?

Lucy *shakes her head.*

Brian   Are you one hundred per cent certain that you're going to pop your self back on that bed and take some nice deep breaths and chill your boots for me.

Lucy *nods.*

Brian   Good.

Lucy   I'll do everything you tell me, I can't stand it any more I can't.

She wants to cry but holds herself in. Silence.

Lucy   I want to change my life. I want to so badly. Please.

Brian *nods.* **Lucy** *calms right down. Silence.*

Brian   I'll do what I can.

Lucy   Thank you. Thank you.

Brian   I'm only doing what my mother always taught me to do best. To be interfering and nosey.

He smiles. **Lucy** *laughs and then smiles a beautiful smile before clouding over again.*

Lucy   Mr Nurse please tell me the number you're talking about, who is it?

Brian   It's Brian.

Lucy   Brian please.

Brian   We've the number of a crisis intervention team. They'll do what they can if they can and give you a bed if they've space.

Lucy   If? No, no, no. No.

Brian   Yes pet. If. If they can do it and you can do it.

Seven

A room in a North London crisis intervention centre three days later. It's pretty basic. A bed, wash basin and a mirror.

Lucy *washes herself in the basin, then brushes her hair and looks in the mirror. She looks and feels better. Silence.*

Marina, *a care worker, enters.*

Marina Lucy?

Lucy Yes?

Marina Didn't you fancy any breakfast?

Lucy No.

Marina Lucy you need to get your strength up.

Lucy I could smell the fried food from here and it made me want to vomit.

Marina You can have toast and fruit juice. There's toast and fruit juice Lucy.

Lucy And no doubt horrible white bread.

Marina You're undernourished and you need three good meals a day while you're here.

Lucy The methadone's made me feel sick. It's disgusting, it's like Nightnurse.

Marina Lucy.

Lucy And are you sure this room is all you have? If you call my mother I'm sure she will pay for the best room.

Marina Lucy there are only thirty rooms here. Serving all of greater London. You're lucky you've one of the only single rooms Lucy.

Lucy Lucky? I don't think so.

Silence.

Marina   Lucy you made an agreement when we admitted you last night to stick by the rules and boundaries we've got. They're for everyone's benefit including you.

Lucy   What, eating a cooked breakfast?

Marina   You need to make sure you go to breakfast. And see everyone Lucy.

Lucy   I don't want to be with all those people.

Marina   Why what's wrong with them?

Lucy   They're all men and the other two women are crack whores. I think I'd rather stay in my cell.

Marina   It's not a cell. I know its strange being here. And everything is new. But you will have a lot more similarities with the other people here than you realise now. And you can learn from other people's insights.

Lucy   I'll thank you if you're finished.

Marina   Your first group is at ten o'clock Lucy.

Lucy   How interesting.

Marina   Lucy you made an agreement to attend groups. Didn't you Lucy?

Lucy   And do what?

Marina   The group work is an important part of the work we do here. Its an important part of how we support you in your time here and to prepare for what comes next. Its like learning a new language. It feels hard at first. But you gain insights into how your mind works and what motivates you. And that knowledge is power Lucy.

Lucy   To do what?

Marina   Get in touch with who you really are. As opposed to the person you think you are and who you think you should be.

Lucy   Oh please.

Marina   You don't have to say anything Lucy. And some things aren't appropriate for group therapy anyway. You don't have to worry about a thing.

Lucy   I'm sorry but I am not one of those people.

Silence.

Marina   Don't put your energy elsewhere Lucy.

Lucy   Oh don't worry I've no intention of putting my energy elsewhere.

Marina   I know how hard it is.

Lucy   I doubt that very much.

Silence.

Marina   All sorts of people share your experiences Lucy.

Lucy   I'm me. I'm my own person.

Silence.

And I must be the biggest freak in the world.

Marina   You're not.

Lucy   I think I must be to end up here.

Silence.

Marina   You're not. Look at me. Mad as a box of frogs I know.

She smiles.

Lucy   I've never been so ashamed in my life, I think I'd rather be dead.

Marina   You're alive Lucy.

Lucy   I think I really would rather be dead and buried.

Marina   We all make bad choices Lucy. Because we're human. We're all in the same boat.

Silence.

Where are you Lucy?

Lucy   Right now I'm in a crummy room in a crisis centre about half a mile from where I –

She wants to cry but she stops herself.

Grew up.

Marina   You're safe here.

Lucy   Am I?

Marina   You are.

Lucy   Am I?

Marina   Yes you are.

Silence.

Lucy   I am so ashamed. It's like a veil, a mist, a fog, a thick fog, a putrid sticky fog that's in my eyes and my ears and my mouth and my nose and every pore of my body and my feet and all over my hands and in my heart and it will never go away never. Please don't make me go out.

Silence.

Marina   And why are you here Lucy?

Lucy   Because my life has become chaotic and out of control and I have been attacked and –

Silence.

And I think my life may now be in danger and other people must agree with me because I am here. Taking a valuable bed. And I had everything I wanted.

She wants to cry but holds herself in.

Lucy   You won't tell anyone who I am will you? You won't tell my mother will you?

Marina   Lucy why are you here?

Lucy   So I can detox so I don't die.

Marina   Why are you here?

Lucy   I don't know why because all I want to do is die. I think it would be better for everyone concerned.

Silence.

Marina   You don't mean that.

Lucy   I do. I do.

Silence.

I really do. What's the point of me being in this world? Why should I live and breathe when I'm of no use to anyone and I'm no more than a never-ending source of danger and utter, utter heartbreak to everyone I know and to myself? I have broken my own heart and I know I will never ever be able to mend it. It is broken.

She wipes some tears away and then gets herself together.

Lucy   Only one bad thing has ever happened in my life until I started smoking heroin. I've only been clean a day and everything is coming back. My head is so full of my own life. It's all coming back. And you know what is so awful? My dad died when I was six months old and apart from that, I don't even remember that, there's not been one bad thing that has happened to me that I can think of that's why. That's why. So it must only be me I'm obviously a born fuck-up. Did I grow up on the Mountford Estate in Hackney? Was my mother a drug addict or prostitute? Did I go to a crappy comp and go on the dole when I was sixteen? Was I bullied or did I have brothers and sisters who hated me? Was I abused? Did I have no talents? I was the star of my year at school.

She sings. She's a blinding singer. It's too much. She bursts into tears. Silence apart from the sound of her crying.

Marina *gives her a tissue.* **Lucy** *wipes her eyes and pulls herself together. Silence.*

Lucy   I can't go to a group. What will they think of me?

Marina   Everyone feels like you.

Lucy   But how can they when I've had so much and they've had nothing?

Marina   It's not like that.

Lucy   I don't think I can do it.

Marina   Why are you here Lucy?

Lucy *blows her nose and thinks.*

Marina   Why did you ring the number after the hospital gave it to you Lucy? Why did you ring us Lucy?

Lucy   Because.

Marina   Because what?

Lucy   Because.

Marina   Because you want to get better. You've spoken to me last night.

Lucy   But you're different.

Marina   You've spoken to me Lucy.

Lucy   It's different there's only one of you.

Marina   I know what you do for a living. You could stand in front of a camera and talk to thousands, millions, if someone asked you.

Lucy   Of children. And I only lasted three episodes before I fucked that one up.

Marina   You and a dozen others is nothing for you Lucy. Nothing.

Lucy   I can't leave this room.

Marina   You can. You're amongst friends and fellow travellers here.

Lucy   Fellow travellers. Smokers of opium.

She smiles and thinks.

Marina   You can do it.

Lucy   If I'm compelled to.

Marina   Not for me. For you. You can do it. You can do it for you. Everything else is background now. It's all static.

Lucy *looks at* **Marina** *directly.*

Marina   This is about you doing all the things you need to do to get yourself better. Not what other people want. What you want. What you need. Where you need to put your energy to go where you need to go.

Silence.

Marina   I'll be outside for a few minutes and we can go up to the group room together if you like. I'll introduce you to everyone. You can do it. You have to do it. I know you can.

Lucy   How?

Marina   Because I've seen a thousand girls like you in my time here. Feeling like the world is coming to an end. And it's hard but – But when they've the determination to effect a change in their life and go for it they do Lucy.

Silence.

I'll be outside.

She nods and goes. Silence.

Lucy *spends as much time thinking about her decision as is conceivably possible, takes a deep breath and walks out of the room.*

Interval.

Eight

A room in the North London crisis intervention centre. There are three plastic chairs.

Barbara *waits nervously on one of them. She checks her watch. Silence.*

Lucy *enters carrying a sports bag. She is accompanied by* **Marina** *who has a folder under her arm.* **Barbara** *stands.*

Barbara Hello Lucy.

Lucy Hi Mum.

Barbara You look well.

Lucy Thanks.

Marina Who let you in?

Barbara A young man.

Marina Well you shouldn't be in here.

Barbara It had started to rain. What do you expect me to do? Stand on the street?

Silence.

You look well Lucy.

Lucy Thank you.

Marina You know she's put on nearly a stone since she's been here.

Barbara Have you?

Lucy I was a bit skinny.

Barbara I made a spaghetti bolognese. Its on the hob.

Lucy Great.

Barbara And in case you didn't fancy that there's macaroni cheese. I made that as well.

Lucy   I don't mind.

Barbara   And I thought you might be hungry so I brought some sandwiches. Cheese and jam. And some crisps as well.

She rifles around in her bag for the sandwiches which she brings out in a tupperware box.

Lucy   I had breakfast.

Barbara   Oh what did you have, I suppose the food's not up to much is it?

Lucy   Mummy that's pretty rude.

Silence.

It's great.

Marina   We don't have a fantastic budget but our chef Gaz works some miracles and we're all convinced its only a matter of time before he's on the box on *Masterchef.*

Barbara   Look I brought Mr Dog.

She puts the sandwiches back in her bag and fetches out an old battered soft toy of a Labrador dog.

Barbara   Look Mr Dog. Mr Dog Lucy.

She gingerly advances towards **Lucy** *with the soft toy.* **Lucy** *doesn't want it.*

Marina   Barbara I'm not sure –

Lucy *takes it and looks at it.* **Barbara** *embraces* **Lucy**.

Marina   Barbara.

Barbara   Sorry, sorry.

She backs away.

Lucy   It's okay.

She goes to her mum and gives her the hug she wants. **Barbara** *wipes her eyes.*

Barbara   Look at you.

Marina   Lucy I think we should pop upstairs and talk privately for ten minutes don't you? I'll get someone to fetch down a coffee for your mum.

Barbara   What about?

Lucy   No.

Silence.

Marina   What is it Lucy?

Lucy   We can talk here.

Barbara   What about?

Lucy   I don't know what happens next.

Barbara   Don't you want to come home?

Silence.

She doesn't want to come home.

Silence.

Lucy   No I do.

Barbara   I love you Lucy.

Lucy   I love you Mummy. I do want to come home.

Marina   Lucy's doing great. She's been a star.

Barbara   She's always been a star you don't need to tell me that.

Marina   But every step takes great courage and strength.

Silence.

Barbara   Angela's coming round at the weekend.

Lucy   Is she?

Barbara   That will be nice won't it?

Lucy   Yes.

Marina   Is Angela your older sister?

Lucy   Yes.

Marina   Would you like to see her?

Lucy   I don't know.

Silence.

Barbara   Things are better.

Lucy   Are they?

Barbara   I contacted Angela.

Lucy   Did you?

Barbara   I've tried to make things up to her Lucy.

Lucy   Have you?

Barbara   I apologised with all my heart.

Silence.

Lucy   What did you say to her?

Barbara   I said sorry.

Lucy   What for?

Barbara   Well I said sorry for – You know. I said sorry.

Lucy   What for?

Barbara *glances at* **Marina**. *Silence.*

Marina   Look I feel – This is an inappropriate situation for me to be in.

Lucy   I want you to stay.

Silence.

Barbara   I feel uncomfortable. I –

Lucy   I think it would be better if I stopped tonight and Mummy can come and collect me tomorrow morning.

Marina   You have stayed for the maximum period already Lucy.

Lucy   Yes, Mummy can come back in the morning.

Marina   Lucy, we're already admitting a girl upstairs in your place.

Lucy   Well you can't.

Silence.

Barbara   Lucy you should see your room.

Lucy   I want to stay here.

Barbara   I went to John Lewis and you've new bedding, its lovely. Not at all girly-girly like your old things. You're a grown woman now. Lucy, we've a taxi booked.

Lucy   Haven't you brought the car up?

Barbara   I didn't know where I would park.

Lucy   Why didn't you drive?

Barbara   A taxi's easier.

Lucy   Why didn't you drive?

Barbara   Because I didn't want to drive.

Silence.

I must say whether I drive or take a taxi has never concerned you before.

Silence.

I do apologise.

Marina   Not at all. Its not an easy thing. For either of you.

Lucy   I don't want to go home.

Marina   I'm afraid I have to get on as well.

Lucy   If I go home I –

Silence.

Marina   You need to put your energy into what's next, not what came before Lucy. None of it matters any more.

Barbara   I've done my homework Lucy.

Lucy   Mummy I can deal with whatever I need to deal with.

Barbara   And you will have my support. I would like to tell the lady here. Or they will think I am a poor mother.

Silence.

Lucy   You're not a poor mother.

Barbara   I feel like a poor mother. I feel like the worst mother in the world.

Marina   You're not chuck.

Barbara   Well it's very hard to believe at the moment. After everything.

She wants to cry but holds herself in.

Marina   I'd recommend you doing FA.

Silence.

Barbara   How dare you speak to me like that. How dare she.

Marina   I'm sorry I think you've got the wrong end of the stick.

Barbara   How dare she say that, who are these people Lucy?

Lucy   She didn't mean fuck all mother. Its Families Anonymous.

Marina   Its an organisation called Families Anonymous. There's CoDA as well.

Barbara   What is that?

Lucy   It's Co-Dependents Anonymous.

Silence.

Barbara   I don't really think that sort of thing is for people like us.

Marina   It's hard for the families to come to terms. Mothers in particular find it very hard that the person you gave birth to and nursed and nourished and brought up has – had the kind of problems Lucy has. You need support.

Barbara   That's quite enough. I won't speak about my family and private life in this way.

Lucy   Mother.

Marina   Look I –

Barbara   I won't. I have come to fetch my daughter home and that is all we need to discuss.

Silence.

As soon as Lucy is home everything will be fine. Won't it darling? Won't it? As I was trying to say I have found a masseur who will come to Gibson Square. And a craniosacral therapist and I thought perhaps we could go to a pilates class together. Couldn't we darling?

Lucy   Yes we could.

Barbara   And I've booked for the two of us and Angela to have a weekend away.

Lucy   The three of us? Together.

Barbara   At a health spa. In Hampshire. In Brockenhurst. In the New Forest. Its not too far from Southampton. If we get fed up we could catch the ferry and go to the Isle of Wight. I've always wanted to go to Osborne House. Of course Queen Victoria died there. 'We are not amused.' Anyway I think it will do us all good. To be away together as a family. I think Angela has stress issues even before one takes into consideration her career in the law. But if you would rather we went together then I'm sure Angela won't mind us going on our own.

Lucy   No.

Marina   Sounds great. I wish someone would take me to Blackpool.

She laughs. **Lucy** *looks at* **Barbara**.

Lucy   Thank you Mummy. That would be lovely. The three of us.

Marina   Well how lovely.

Barbara   Honestly darling I will speak to Angela if you don't want her there.

Lucy   No, I'd like her to be there.

Barbara   Whatever you want.

Silence.

Lucy   Will you be honest?

Barbara   About what?

Lucy   I don't know.

Barbara   Darling you know there are no secrets between us.

Silence.

Lucy   I suppose we ought be going home?

Marina   Yes I think it's time to say goodbye.

Lucy   Goodbye Marina.

Marina   Goodbye. You can be very proud of everything you've achieved here.

Lucy   It doesn't feel like three weeks.

Marina   Everyone says that.

Lucy   It feels like a lifetime.

Silence.

Barbara   Thank you for helping my daughter.

Marina   We do what we can.

Barbara   I mean it sincerely.

Marina   I know you do. Here before you go. Did you hear the one about the morbidly obese junkie?

Barbara *glances at* **Lucy** *uncertainly.*

Marina   When he fell over he tried to smoke the crack he made in the pavement.

She laughs.

Marina   Oh don't get me started we'll be here all day.

Lucy *laughs and gives* **Marina** *a little wave.*

Marina   I hope you won't be offended when I say I hope I never see you again.

Lucy   Don't worry Marina. I'm never coming back.

Nine

Lucy *sits opposite* **Dr Harris** *in his room in the drug treatment centre at a large North London hospital. There is a bed where patients can be examined in the room.*

Dr Harris *has a questionnaire resting on the inch-thick yellow folder containing* **Lucy**'s *notes. He has a pen ready to write. He takes notes through the consultation.*

Lucy   Where's Dr Burden-Rogers?

Dr Harris   I'm afraid Dr. Burden-Rogers is away. I'm Dr Harris, Dr Burden-Rogers' SHO.

Lucy   Is he on holiday?

Dr Harris   He's at a conference in Malta. Anyway, shall we begin?

Lucy *stands up and gathers her bag as if to leave.*

Lucy   I'll wait until he comes back.

Dr Harris   Now we've not met before I know, but why don't you sit down and tell me a little bit about yourself?

Lucy   If you want to know about me why don't you read my fucking notes.

Silence.

Dr Harris   I have read your notes Lucy. You're doing remarkably well. It would be great to hear where you're at. In your own words. I think it's important don't you?

Lucy   I'm on methadone.

Dr Harris   How much?

Lucy   Seventy milligrams.

Dr Harris   How often do you pick up?

Lucy   Once a week.

Dr Harris   How do you feel about that?

Lucy   Okay.

Dr Harris   That's great.

Lucy   I used to be on supervised consumption but now I just pick up once a week.

Dr Harris   Now you're twenty-nine and you're single is that correct?

Lucy   Yes it is. Thanks for the little reminder.

Silence.

Dr Harris   And where do you live?

Lucy   With my mother in Islington,

Dr Harris   And no children?

Lucy   No. No children.

Silence.

Dr Harris   And do you use anything on top of the methadone?

Lucy   No.

Dr Harris   No alcohol or cannabis? Do you smoke?

Lucy   Yes.

Dr Harris   How many per day would you say you smoke?

Lucy   I don't keep count.

Dr Harris   Ten? A small pack?

Lucy   I didn't realise I was here because of my self-destructive relationship with Mr Marlboro Light.

Silence.

Dr Harris   Any crack? Or heroin on top? Perhaps for a treat.

Lucy   Nothing for ages.

Dr Harris   Ages?

Lucy   Maybe once a month.

Dr Harris   Do you inject?

Lucy   No. Listen Dr Twat why don't you read my notes?

Dr Harris   I know it's a bit tedious Lucy but you've been through a review before and you know the form. We need a thorough interview. Now if I can recall, you haven't injected for approximately a year is that correct?

Lucy   Yes.

Dr Harris   And you have a little on top as a treat once monthly.

Lucy   It's not a treat.

Dr Harris   Yes?

Lucy   It's more like a visceral whole body yearning for something exciting in my excruciatingly boring new life. My daily treat is now *Loose Women* and I never thought I'd say that about that bunch of third-rate harridans.

Dr Harris *laughs. Silence.*

Dr Harris   So you smoke it off of foil?

Lucy   Yes I do.

Dr Harris   How do you pay for it?

Silence.

Lucy   I don't. My mother pays for it.

Dr Harris   And where do you get it?

Lucy   My mother meets my dealer in a little cafe on Upper Street. And you know she sometimes buys him a cake. Apparently he's fond of meringues.

Silence.

Dr Harris   And how's your health in general?

Lucy   Okay. I think.

Dr Harris   And how are you getting on with the interferon injections?

Lucy   Glad it's over that's for sure.

Dr Harris   Oh you've finished the treatment?

Lucy   Yeah, six months of the evil fucker.

Dr Harris   And the hepatitis C?

Lucy   It's cured. I've got one more blood test. But it's gone. I know it's gone.

She smiles. So does **Dr Harris**.

Dr Harris   Why don't you sit down? I assure you while you may think I'm a twat I'm actually quite a nice bloke.

Lucy   I'll be the judge of that.

Dr Harris *smiles.* **Lucy** *thinks and then goes back to her chair.*

Lucy   You're okay. I can see you're okay.

Dr Harris   Thank you.

He smiles.

Lucy   That's okay.

Dr Harris   So how are you feeling about your treatment? Where are you hoping to get to next Lucy?

Lucy *thinks. She is very serious.*

Lucy   I want to get my methadone script cut down. I want to come off it as soon as I can. I want to get back to work. I want to get my life back. I want to get back to work. It's so boring. It's so boring. I want to be a normal person like you again. I want to get back to work and get my own place and do all the things I've always thought about doing. I need to. I want my dignity. It is so important to me. I have to do this. I will be too old. I want to be completely clean from everything before I'm thirty.

Silence.

Do you know how much the little children adore the *Animal Show*? Do you? They won't understand why I've gone. And I miss them.

Silence.

Dr Harris   Yes. I can see how much this means. And you say your mother buys the heroin when you have a little bit as a treat?

Lucy   And? She doesn't want me getting mixed up with dealers any more. What's wrong with that? It makes sense for her and it works for me. I don't want to mix with them either.

Silence.

Dr Harris   And the last proper relapse was six months ago?

Lucy   More of a lapse I'd say. Not a relapse. I didn't inject.

Silence.

Dr Harris   Lucy we don't want to run before we can walk and –

Lucy   Have you read my notes? Really? I am tired of this life. I am tired of getting clean, lapsing, getting clean, relapsing, getting clean and relapsing. I am on the road. And I am not going back. I am never going back. I want to detox completely.

Silence.

Dr Harris   Well we can't force you to do anything. This is about you.

Lucy   I need to get back to work. I need to pay my own way and get back in to my flat. I need to get my life back. I know I do.

Silence.

Dr Harris   And what is your relationship with your former employers?

Lucy   They said once I sorted myself out we could have a conversation about coming back.

Dr Harris   And how likely do you think it is they will honour that understanding?

Lucy   Listen if I can be blunt those fuckers hushed it up and if they don't want to be nice then I will make trouble for them.

Dr Harris   I see. So your employment status is –

Lucy   Resting.

Dr Harris *makes some notes. Silence.*

Lucy   You know an important staging post in my sexual development was an adolescent fantasy I had of being fucked over a desk by a doctor in a white coat.

Dr Harris *looks up alarmed.*

Lucy   Joke. Joke.

Dr Harris *laughs exceedingly nervously and dives back into his notes.*

Dr Harris   You said you were living with your mother?

Lucy   Yes.

Dr. Harris   And there's no one else there?

Lucy   No.

Dr Harris   And does she work?

Lucy   She's got savings.

Dr Harris   So you live off your mother's savings?

Lucy   I don't want to talk about my mother any more today.

Dr Harris   And where is your father?

Lucy   He's dead.

Dr Harris   How did he die?

Lucy   I don't want to talk about my mother and my father.

Dr Harris   Do you have any siblings?

Lucy   I have a sister Angela and she's a solicitor and that's about it.

She stands.

Dr Harris   I just want to understand if there's anything in the family that might be of relevance. Any predisposition.

Lucy   What to being a junkie and a fuck-up?

Dr Harris   If you want to put it like that.

Lucy *smiles.*

Dr Harris   So there's no history of any prescription drugs. Alcohol. Anything like that in the family?

Lucy *thinks, smiles.*

Lucy   No. But grandfather fell off the side of a tug boat in the war after drinking too much rum. The old sea dog.

Dr Harris   I can see you share a sense of humour with Dr Burden-Rogers.

Lucy   Yes he doesn't hide behind his questionnaire as much as you.

She smiles.

Dr Harris   You're aggressive. Angry. Why is that?

Lucy   You're the psychiatrist. You tell me.

Silence.

I like Dr Burden-Rogers. He gives me the horn.

She smiles. Silence.

Dr Harris   Now I noticed in your last medical review there were multiple deliberate self-harming events.

Lucy *bursts out laughing.*

Lucy   Go on say that again.

Dr Harris   In your last medical review it was noted there were multiple deliberate self-harming events.

Lucy   That is so *Grey's Anatomy*.

Dr Harris   I'm glad to be a source of such amusement.

Lucy   You are.

Dr Harris   Are you still cutting?

Lucy   You really should lighten up.

Dr Harris *checks his questionnaire. Silence.*

Dr Harris   Nothing criminal. No. Well I suppose – Ahem.

Lucy   No. Nothing for ages.

Dr Harris   You look well.

Lucy   Why thank you kind sir.

Dr Harris   You seem pretty together.

Lucy   I feel more like myself.

Silence.

Dr Harris   Now Lucy I want to talk to you a little bit more about how you're feeling. If I were to say that one out of ten is feeling very low indeed. So as one might feel everything were completely pointless. And ten out of ten were say one of the best days where you feel really good. How many out of ten would you say you feel now?

Lucy   About five. Maybe five and a half.

Dr Harris   Well that's a first, a client using a half point.

Dr Harris *laughs. Silence.*

Lucy   Groovy.

Dr Harris   And would you say you've felt better or worse than five point five in the last month say?

Lucy   Worse.

Dr Harris   And how many out of ten would you say?

Lucy   One.

Dr Harris   One?

Lucy   Point five.

Dr Harris   And would say you felt life –

Lucy   Wasn't worth living? Yes I would. But one must have hope wouldn't you say Dr Harris?

Dr Harris   Yes I would.

Lucy   That's my point five.

Silence.

Dr Harris   Is anything worrying you?

Lucy   I need to get back to work. You know my career. It's the most important thing.

Dr Harris   Yes I understand. Any anxiety? Panic attacks?

Lucy   Yes.

Dr Harris   How often would you say?

Lucy   Maybe once a fortnight.

Dr Harris   Good. Do you ever have any thoughts you can't get out of your head or do you ever worry about anything, which actually if you looked at the facts, you might not be so worried about? Do you understand what I mean?

Lucy   Welcome to my world.

She laughs. So does **Dr Harris**.

Dr Harris   Is there anything which recurs?

Lucy   No.

Silence.

Dr Harris   Well. Let's get the nurse in and do the physical examination and you can get off home to *Loose Women*.

He realises he's said the wrong thing and goes to the door and calls for the nurse.

Eileen.

He looks at **Lucy**.

Dr Harris   I don't think now is the time to try a complete detox. I think you're doing very well but –

Lucy   I don't feel I'm going anywhere. I'm so bored.

Dr Harris   I think it's vitally important we sustain the new stability in your life. You have done so well Lucy.

Lucy *blushes. She doesn't know why.*

Dr Harris   Have I said something?

Lucy *finds courage.*

Dr Harris   Yes?

Lucy   There was one thing.

Dr Harris   Go on.

Lucy   After my first relapse my mother got rid of our masseur when I scored some weed from him. But she still retains this faith in manipulating my body. In touching me.

Dr Harris   Touching you?

Lucy   No not in a dirty way. Or an abusive way. But she insists on rubbing and massaging my feet. As if she were Aladdin. As if she could wish my illness away.

Silence.

I can't stand to have my feet touched. I never have. I was so ticklish as a child. You've no need to examine my feet. I've never injected into my feet. I couldn't bear it. I once had a boyfriend who thought the height of erotic sophistication was to lick my feet clean. In the end I burst a blood vessel in his eye because I reacted reflexively. And kicked him the face.

Dr Harris *smiles.*

Lucy   It's my mother. When she touches my feet I feel so intensely awkward I shut my eyes and I almost go out of my body I feel so uncomfortable. She thinks she's induced a healing trance which of course only encourages her. But I imagine her eating me. The tendon. Lower tibia. A great lump of calf muscle and the burst femoral vein hosing us both down in arterial blood. I often think if my mother could she would eat me. Eat me whole. So she could have me back in her tummy again.

Dr Harris   I see.

He hesitates, unsure whether to make a further note now.

Lucy   These are the thoughts that come into my head Dr Harris. And they simply won't go away. I don't think they will. Not while I'm on drugs. And methadone is a drug. Like heroin is a drug. I need to be free of everything before I can get myself sane.

Dr Harris   I don't think you should go it alone.

Lucy   I don't think Dr Burden-Rogers would agree with you there Dr Harris. I really don't. He knows me.

Dr Harris   I don't think any doctor worth his salt would endorse such a risky course of action.

Lucy *thinks.*

Lucy   I've made my mind up. And there's nothing you could say that would change my mind.

Ten

A room in the North London crisis intervention centre. There are three plastic chairs.

Barbara *stands and so does* **Lucy** *and* **Marina**. *There's tension between them. Silence.*

Lucy   I'm not coming home with you this time Mother.

Silence.

Marina   We have a lot of dealings with the hostel.

Barbara   The hostel.

Lucy   I don't know why you have come.

Barbara   I am your mother.

Lucy   Didn't you read my letter?

Barbara   Yes but I thought I could give you a lift.

Marina   I know this is difficult Barbara.

Barbara   Difficult?

Silence.

My dear I'm not sure there's a word in the English language which is adequate to describe what it's been like in the last two and a half years.

Silence.

Lucy   You're driving?

Barbara   Yes.

Lucy   Are you sure you should be driving?

Barbara   Yes.

Lucy   Mummy I think I need to try and stand on my own two feet.

Barbara   On your own two feet?

Lucy   Yes.

Silence.

Barbara   Why?

Lucy   I just do.

Barbara   But how is going to live in a hostel going to help you?

Marina   Lucy's care worker will be coming to collect her.

Barbara   Her care worker?

Silence.

I don't understand this. I know after your father died perhaps I over-compensated with you. You never knew him in the way Angela did. But I can't see for the life of me what I have done wrong. As a mother. Except to try and give you the most magical childhood and love you and look after you.

Silence.

I dare say there's not a girl in London who had a dressing-up box to compare with yours.

Silence.

Lucy   I am very grateful.

Barbara   I can't get over it. She was such a brilliant girl. You should have heard the stories she came up with. Lucy and Mr Dog on the bus up to the Heath. So funny and entertaining. Off the wall and yet incredibly considerate and affectionate. The cuddles we had. Actually until the last few years. I miss it terribly. I miss you darling. I miss you so much.

Silence.

No matter how many times I go over and over this in my mind I –

Lucy   And what about what I want?

Marina   After Lucy tried to stop taking her methadone it was a significant relapse she had. A real setback for her. She doesn't want to go backwards like that again. I think Lucy feels that coming home now is too much to deal with all at once after relapsing and detoxing this time.

Barbara   I know what Lucy feels, I have read her letter.

Silence.

How can a mother and mother's love be too much?

Silence.

Lucy if you go and live in a hostel how on earth are you going to get back to work?

Lucy   I will manage.

Barbara   They won't take you back. No one will have you. How will you keep your clothes and make yourself presentable? People will know.

Lucy *looks at* **Marina**. *Silence.*

Lucy   I would like to come home, but I'm afraid.

Barbara   Afraid of what? I'll do anything you want.

Lucy   I don't want you to do anything I want. I want you to say no. I want you to say no.

Silence.

Barbara   I have only ever done what you have asked me to do.

Lucy   But Mother you have brought me drugs when I have asked you to pay for them and pick them up.

Silence.

Barbara   What would you do?

Silence.

Would you see your daughter. Your precious daughter go onto the streets and prostitute herself?

Silence.

Would you rather have a phone call in the middle of the night from your daughter screaming her dealer is going to kill her. And the phone go dead. And not sleep for a week believing she is lying dead in an alleyway. Or would you rather she was safe at home in her bedroom?

Silence.

Please tell me Lucy what would you do?

Silence.

Would you rather your daughter have clean needles or would you rather she contracted hepatitis C or HIV?

Lucy   But Mummy you enable my habit.

Barbara   I would give anything. I would give my life if we could only turn back the clock to the very first time I caught you and your friends smoking pot. I've gone over and over it in my head. I thought she's only thirteen. Her sister's at university. She hasn't got anyone. Only me. Her friends. And should I force those good children? From good families with their whole lives ahead of them onto the street corners. Prone to tough kids pushing harder drugs upon them. In danger of arrest.

Silence.

And God darling I did drugs when I was young. It was the sixties. Don't you think I wish I had done things differently? But I am only trying to do my best. But whatever my best is it is the wrong thing.

Silence.

You can come home and I don't mind if you completely shut me out. Just ignore me. We can live separately. Only come home. Come home darling. Let me look after you.

Lucy *looks at* **Marina**. *Silence.*

Marina   Lucy's decided what she wants to do. I know it must be very painful.

Lucy   No I haven't.

Silence.

Barbara   Are you going to come home?

Silence.

Lucy   You must make a promise.

Barbara   I would make a promise in my own blood.

Silence.

Lucy   You must never ever enable my habit again. No matter how much I beg, scream and fight.

Barbara   I won't.

Lucy   And most importantly of all.

Silence.

Barbara   Yes darling? Tell me. You can tell me. You know you can.

Silence.

Lucy   You must always say no. Especially when I threaten that I'm going to leave home.

Silence.

Barbara *nods her head and then holds out her arms.*

Eleven

A quiet corner in a cafe on Upper Street, Islington. A table and two chairs, a pot of tea, milk jug and crockery for two.

Lucy *stands as a man in a smart suit with a briefcase enters. This is* **Andrew**.

Lucy   Are you Andrew?

Andrew   Yes I am. I'm sorry I'm a few minutes late.

Lucy   Please. Sit down.

Andrew   Great.

Lucy   I've a pot of tea. But would you like some coffee?

Andrew   No tea's fine. Thank you.

He sits down.

Lucy   Thank you for coming over.

Andrew   Oh it's no trouble..

Lucy   I don't like to stray too far from home at the moment.

Andrew   Yes I hear you've been ill?

Lucy   Yes I have. But I'm much better now. Much more like my old self.

Andrew *fiddles around with his case which he then leaves on the table.*

Lucy   Shall I put it on the floor?

Andrew   Oh no I had my laptop bag stolen a few weeks ago and I'm a touch paranoid at the moment.

Lucy   Oh I'm so sorry to hear that.

Andrew   Anyway thank you for meeting me.

Lucy   Oh no the pleasure is all mine.

Andrew   You were rather hard to track down. I understand you're not with your agent any more?

Lucy   Oh well there wasn't any point. I wasn't well. And anyway she never did much for me and I'm forever getting calls from people desperate to represent me. God it can be such a pain. So I haven't heard of your company or your good self before but I understand you're producing a show and you're looking for someone to present it?

Andrew   We're interested in meeting people. Talking to people.

Lucy   But you're meeting people right?

Andrew   God I loved the *Animal House* when you were on it. And my nieces and nephews loved it. And you know the thing that really made me laugh was I'd be in the gym on the cross-trainer in the morning. And you'd have Sky News, and Sky Sports News, and BBC Breakfast, and MTV but you'd have a dozen men all watching you on CBBC. I thought this girl is going to go all the way. Davina. Dermot. Watch out. I did. I still do.

Lucy *laughs and blushes a bit. Silence.*

Lucy   I really loved it. I miss it.

Andrew   Three years ago wasn't it?

Lucy   Doesn't time fly?

Andrew   So what exactly happened?

Silence.

Lucy   Well.

Andrew   I mean obviously I know what was said publicly. That you'd had some kind of breakdown. And there were all sorts of rumours that you'd completely lost the plot and been wandering around the streets. I mean. I know. Things get exaggerated. And I suppose I need to know where I am. Before we can take this discussion any further.

Lucy   Right.

Andrew   And there were other rumours that things had been hushed up. At the BBC. That the Exec had decided to keep something quiet.

Lucy   Right.

Andrew   Television is. It's a small world. And people talk. And I feel I need to know the truth whatever it is. Because those boys in the tabloid press can be such utter shits when they get their teeth in to someone.

Silence.

I'd love to work with you.

Lucy   So would I.

Andrew   And what we've got is a great new format for a kids' nature show. Lot of travel. *Animal House* can kiss their fucking BAFTA goodbye.

Lucy   It's a nature show?

Silence.

Andrew   So Lucy? What gives?

Lucy   You know I want to get back to work. It's all I've ever wanted.

Andrew   We have to be honest with each other.

Lucy   Yes I can see that.

Andrew   So we can defend your side of the story.

Lucy   Yes.

Andrew   Should it ever come out.

Lucy   I don't think it will. It's been over three years.

Silence.

Lucy   And anyway I've been doing this thing recently. In the last few months. To help me with my illness. And its all about honesty and moral rigour really.

Andrew   Right.

Lucy   I've been going to NA.

Andrew   Sorry could you say that again?

Lucy   Narcotics Anonymous.

Andrew   So you've had a problem with drugs?

Lucy   Yes.

Silence.

Andrew   I'm not judging you.

Lucy   Thank you. It's important.

Andrew   So the BBC hushed it up?

Lucy   The Exec did. I don't think anyone knew above him. And it wasn't like many people knew who I was. He knew he should have played it by the book and hung me out to dry but he didn't. He called me shortly after and he was very keen I kept quiet obviously. And he promised me as soon as I was feeling better I could call him and he'd make sure I was looked after.

Andrew   And this is the man who's now in charge of children's television?

Lucy   With me fronting your new show I wouldn't have thought you would have any problem getting it commissioned? Would you?

Andrew *can't believe his luck and laughs. Silence.*

He studies her.

Lucy   You haven't changed your mind have you? Because I really need this.

Andrew   It kind of freaked me out a bit when you said it was an illness.

Lucy   Why? It is!

Andrew   I mean you can't really call it an illness can you? It's an addiction.

Lucy   I thought you said you wouldn't judge me?

Andrew   I said I wasn't judging you I didn't say I wouldn't ever judge you.

Lucy   Look are we still having an interview for a job or is something else happening here?

Andrew   You know it's pretty hot to handle what you've just told me. I mean the BBC hush up a drug-taking children's TV presenter, who according to obviously true rumours, was caught red-handed injecting heroin in her dressing room.

Lucy   I was smoking it.

Andrew   Oh well that makes all the difference.

Silence.

Come on you've got to admit it, it's not a real illness.

Lucy   No.

Andrew   It's a make-believe illness.

Lucy   What I've experienced is not make-believe.

Andrew   Apart from the lemming as far as I know humans are the only creatures capable of self-destruction.

Lucy   Lemmings don't throw themselves off cliffs deliberately. That's a widespread misconception.

Andrew   You seem to know a lot about it.

Lucy   Well I had a nature show on the television.

Silence.

Andrew   Come on, it's not a real illness is it? Getting off of your face to try and block out all of life's difficulties and obstacles.

Lucy   Why are you picking an argument with me about this?

Andrew   I mean and it's make-believe the idea that you can treat people any more than it's a real illness in the first place. Taking up all the resources that could be better spent on people with real illnesses. Like cancer. My mother died from cancer. What would you say to her about that?

Lucy   I didn't take up all that many resources, my mother paid for private until – I –

Andrew   Until the money ran out?

Lucy   If it were not for all the support and treatment I have had I would be dead.

Andrew   Can I quote you on that?

Silence.

Lucy   Who the fuck are you?

She stands.

Lucy   Who the fucking Christ are you?

Andrew   Sit down. I. Sit down. And I will explain.

Lucy   Who the fuck are you?

Andrew   Please Lucy.

Silence.

I do work in the media.

He stands.

I work for a well-known popular Sunday newspaper. The news desk had a call.

Silence.

I suggest you sit down. We're not after you.

Lucy *picks up her cup and throws tea over Andrew.*

Andrew   Well thank you very much.

Lucy   The pleasure was all mine. You complete fucking bastard.

Twelve

Lucy *and* **Angela** *stand together in a bar in North London.*

It's a Tuesday night, so the bar is quiet. **Angela** *gulps red wine from the large glass she's drinking from.* **Lucy** *has a Diet Coke.*

Angela What do you want Lucy?

Lucy I need to talk.

Angela Oh you need me?

Lucy I'd like you to allow me to talk to you.

Angela Well Lucy I am all ears.

Silence.

Lucy You're drinking?

Angela Oh for God's sake please. If you can't beat them join them.

Lucy I – I'm sorry.

Angela So am I dear.

Lucy I know you're angry with me about everything. I want to try.

Angela Look let's not mince words. What do you want?

Silence.

Lucy I'm in NA. I've been doing okay. I want to say sorry and make amends for what I've done. It's an important part of it. Truly sister.

Silence.

Lucy I've been going to church. You can pulverise me with your debating skills. As per usual. If you like. And I must admit I feel something of a hypocrite. But there are plenty of women there who don't give a fig about God either, they want to get their kids in good schools.

Silence.

It's something to do on a Sunday. I like the walk to church. I like to sing. Loudly.

Silence.

I've been exploring quite a few things. Hinduism. Buddhism. A number of other eastern traditions as well. You know in Sanskrit there's a phrase *Hridaya-granthi*. It means the knot of the heart. It's meant something to me. The knot of the heart must be broken. In order for self-knowledge. Enlightenment. I've come to realise a heart is easier to break than a knot.

Angela   Yes.

Silence.

Lucy   I thought we would both be married and have children by now. By the time we were this age.

Angela   So did I.

Silence.

Lucy   When I was a kid you gave me the best cuddles. Much nicer than Mummy. I was so lonely when you went to university. I think I cried myself to sleep for a week.

Silence.

I am truly sorry for everything I have done.

She takes a piece of folded paper from her pocket. She passes it to **Angela**. **Angela** *takes it and looks at it.* **Lucy** *has written on both sides.*

Angela   And am I supposed to read this now or take it home to study?

Lucy   I've written down everything I can remember.

Angela *looks at it, turns over the pages and skims it in fifteen seconds.*

Angela   This is no good.

Lucy   What?

Angela   Do you really think everything began when I caught you trying to steal money from my purse in Mum's kitchen?

Silence.

Lucy   No. Of course not.

Angela   But that's where you begin!

Silence.

Lucy   Then perhaps we ought to meet another time when I've had a chance to think about our relationship again. I'm sorry.

Angela   Oh no I've no intention of us meeting again.

Lucy   I can only say I hope you don't mean that.

Silence.

I understand we've become estranged from each other. I do. And in a way we no longer know each other. I don't know you. I haven't taken the time to be interested in your life. I know that. I haven't been able to. But I'm the new me. I'm the new Lucy. And I know you can't possibly imagine everything I've been through.

Angela *goes to drink. Decides not to take a sip.*

Lucy   You don't know what's been going on with me.

Angela   You couldn't be more mistaken.

Silence.

Lucy   I know there's a part of you that knows exactly. Because you cut yourself don't you? Like me.

Angela *is gob-smacked.*

Lucy   I saw you when I was ten years old. You were home for the weekend. And I looked in your room. The door was ajar and I looked in. And you were cutting yourself. Inside your thighs. Watching the blood. Feeling purged. Like you'd just had the best hit of your life. And it's still going on isn't it Angela? Did you think I wouldn't notice the blood on your blouse. That you could explain it away with some excuse or other about menstrual blood. Or as an old stain. When really you went in to the toilet earlier for your fix. You took the razor blade from your purse and you cut your tummy.

Angela   Liar!

Lucy   You know once years ago when I was still at Italia Conti and you had a party to celebrate your new job. In a rare moment of drunken indiscretion Angela, you said you couldn't stand to have a bloke go down on you. Well she wouldn't would she. She wouldn't want him to see what an awful mess she's made of her inner thighs.

Angela   I'm afraid you're very much mistaken.

Silence.

Lucy   I'm very sorry that you say I am. I saw you. And I learned what to do when I was sad.

Angela   Fuck off.

*She gives **Lucy** back the piece of paper with **Lucy**'s story of their relationship.*

Lucy   Would it help if I were to explain what's been going on?

Angela   That would be pointless.

Lucy   Please Angela I am trying.

Angela *explodes.*

Angela   Don't you think I don't know every detail of your life. I have been consumed by it.

She drinks.

Lucy   Angela we can't make a scene in here.

Angela   Then let's go out onto the street.

Lucy   I won't get in to some sort of unseemly slanging match in a bar.

Angela   Why, in case it gets into the newspapers?

Lucy   Angela.

Angela   What a shame it all had to come out? I only wish it happened three years earlier. I wish it had. I wish it had. Perhaps it might have shamed you into stopping. Shamed Mummy from burning through half a million pounds of savings and accumulating another quarter of a million in debt.

Silence.

But no. No. We all have to protect Lucy. Pretty Lucy. Lucy the pretty one. Lucy the talented one. Lucy with the voice of an angel. How straight her back as she adopts the first position. My, look at her plié.

Lucy   I'm not sure how being humiliated in the press and causing a scandal at the BBC has helped anyone, least of all me.

Angela   If you're still maintaining the delusion that you have or ever did have any chance of a career in television again, then I don't believe you are better.

Lucy   I am better. But how you can think all that tabloid hideousness helps me in any way. My career is over.

Angela   Well there's always *Dancing on Ice*.

Silence.

Grow up. It's a make-believe career. It always was. And even then it wasn't make-believe enough. You had to inure it with some moronic faux-rakish behaviour that might have been laughable if it hadn't destroyed what was left of our family. Smokers of opium how ridiculous. I would laugh if I didn't feel so sick. It was good while it lasted but it is gone and you have to face reality.

Silence.

Lucy   Angela you chose the law and I chose entertainment and I don't criticise your choice.

Angela   But was it your choice? Was it mine?

Lucy   I don't know what you mean.

Angela   I was always the intelligent plain one. You were always the pretty and creative one. Who told us that? When really we were both children who had different talents and different needs.

Silence.

Lucy   Was it really that much money? Is Mum really in that much debt because of me?

Silence.

Angela   I rang the news desk.

Lucy   I beg your pardon.

Angela   I tipped off the newspaper.

Lucy   How could you? How could you?

She hangs her head. Silence.

Angela   Very easily having played second fiddle to you for the last thirty years. The last three of which you seem to have been intent on killing yourself.

Silence.

One must always try to put anger to good use. I hoped. I think I've given you a new beginning.

Silence.

Lucy   Perhaps it isn't hate. Perhaps it's love.

Silence.

Angela   Chrissie Hynde knew it.

Lucy Don't, you'll sound like Mother. I think I might fall over. No I'm okay. I'm okay.

Angela *drinks. Silence.*

Angela For what it's worth I'm sorry if I have made the last few weeks difficult.

Lucy Thank you. For telling me the truth.

Silence.

Angela I've missed you.

Lucy I've missed you. Truly.

Silence.

Angela Have you honestly ever talked to Mum? About problems and stuff? I mean ever.

Lucy No. Have you?

Angela No.

Silence.

Lucy Why are the three of us so screwed up?

Angela I feel sorry for Mum losing Dad when we were little but –

Lucy Don't judge her. Don't blame her Angela.

Angela But she –

Lucy This is about me. Its about what I've done. I was the addict. I've blown all the money. I've done all the terrible things. Me. Me. I don't want excuses from you Angela for everything I've done any more than I want them from Mum any more.

Silence.

I am doing my best to make things right with the world, and my family and in me. Please don't take it away from me. This is about me.

Angela *smiles. Silence.*

Angela   But there is something else Lucy.

Lucy   Don't judge her. The world's not black and white. Everyone makes bad choices.

Silence.

Angela   There was something else you don't know. Now you're stronger I think it's time you knew the truth.

Silence.

Lucy   Go on. Well tell me.

Angela   The thing that no one talks about.

Lucy   Which thing?

Angela   You know.

Lucy   Mummy or Daddy?

Angela   Well both of them.

Silence.

Lucy   What is it?

Angela *takes one almighty gulp which finishes her red wine. And smiles kindly at her sister.*

Angela   The big thing. That no one ever talks about. How Daddy died.

Thirteen

The garden of **Barbara**'s *large Islington home.*

It's warm. **Lucy** *has a glass of red wine.* **Barbara**, *who has been gardening, walks towards her and takes the glass. She has a good gulp of the red wine. Lucy lights up a cigarette.*

Barbara   You're smoking darling?

Silence.

Lucy   I know.

Barbara   Well I suppose we all have our little sins.

Lucy   We do.

Barbara   Now do you fancy finishing the French onion soup or shall we have a light salad?

Lucy   A salad will be fine.

Barbara   Are you off out?

Lucy   In a while.

Barbara   Oh you didn't say?

Lucy   That's because I'm leaving. And I thought it would be much harder for both of us if I …

Silence.

Barbara   Isn't the garden looking marvellous. Who would have thought it after all these years? I actually thought someone must have painted the plinth at some point. But you know it was utterly coated in bird shit.

Silence.

Lucy   I love you Mummy.

Barbara   I love you Lucy.

Lucy   Mummy I –

Barbara   Well that explains it. Why the garden was calling.

She wipes her eyes. Silence.

Of course I knew that one day – And here it is.

Silence.

You know the house is going to have to be sold.

Lucy   I will find a way of paying you back.

Barbara   Darling.

Lucy   I will.

Barbara   No. Well anyway. For all of Angela's splendid work with my many and various creditors I don't think they will be kept at bay for much longer. Surely you could wait until then?

Silence.

Lucy   No I can't. I've spent a month thinking very carefully about it. Making my decision. I had a talk with Angela.

Barbara   What has she said?

She drinks. Silence.

Barbara   You know once when I found you.

Lucy   Yes?

Barbara   When I found you in a state.

Lucy   Yes?

Barbara   You said to me that you had a need. You needed something for such a long time. And you had found it. In your state of oblivion. Perhaps you don't remember?

Lucy   I do remember.

Barbara   Of course it's your father. I assume. And I feel so awful about it because –

Lucy   No Mum.

Barbara   No?

Lucy   How can you miss someone you have never known?

Silence.

Barbara   You don't mind me asking do you?

Lucy   No.

Barbara   A mother longs to know these things.

Silence.

Why did you do it? Why did you follow that path? Please tell me.

Lucy   It was something friends were doing. It was something I wanted to be near.

Barbara   But why?

Lucy   I had incredible nerves. I had the most paralysing nerves. Before I go in front of the camera. Smoking weed was impossible. But heroin helped.

Silence.

Barbara   But you've always been so confident?

Lucy   I have always wanted to be so perfect.

Barbara   But why?

Lucy   For you.

Barbara   For me?

Lucy   Because you were so perfect. You gave me everything I ever wanted and made all my dreams come true. I have always been terrified of letting you down.

Silence.

Barbara   But I would not care.

Lucy   But I would.

Barbara   I don't understand.

Lucy   And yet there is a part of me – Have you never been into a beautiful room and wanted to trash it? To move the symmetrically arranged cushions? I once had to meet someone in a suite in the Sanderson. And all I hoped was to come on my period. And I was due. So I could leave a mess in the lavatory. Smack sorted everything out. To begin with.

Silence.

Barbara *drinks.*

Lucy You know detoxing from heroin has never killed anyone but you can die withdrawing from alcohol suddenly. Can't you mother?

Barbara I've no idea what you're talking about.

Silence.

Lucy Angela told me.

Barbara Told you what?

Lucy Angela found out herself quite by accident from old Dr Dennis seven years ago, didn't she mother?

Barbara I don't know what you're getting at.

Lucy You told us Daddy died from a heart attack.

Barbara Which he did.

Lucy Brought on by a, a seizure.

Silence.

He had a problem didn't he?

Barbara He was a good man.

Lucy And you'd stopped drinking because you were carrying me.

Barbara Well that's what happens when you're pregnant Lucy, so I suppose so.

Lucy But Daddy couldn't stop could he?

Barbara Really this is fantasy.

Lucy Because he was addicted. Did you clean up his piss?

Barbara You're becoming more like Angela as you get older.

Lucy But you said you would leave him. You said if he didn't stop drinking right away you were leaving. And he did. He quit. Like that. And he dropped down dead.

Barbara Well I've no idea where you've got all this. I have no idea why Angela would say such a thing.

Lucy You told her when she came round from seeing Dr Dennis to have it out with you. Or don't you remember because you were blind drunk at the time?

Silence.

Is this why you do it? Is it? Is this why you have never been able to put your foot down?

Silence.

Barbara I wanted to protect you. It was so unnecessary.

Lucy What, telling your daughters the truth?

Barbara He – Your father wasn't destructive. He was whacky to Angela. She adored him. But she was growing up and beginning to notice her father's behaviour wasn't normal. And I had you. I didn't want to cloud your lives with any unnecessary darkness after he died.

Lucy The world is full of light and dark mother!

Barbara I wanted you to have all the love two parents could give.

Lucy And left Angela with none.

Barbara That isn't true. I admit you were my favourite.

Lucy Why did you try to make Angela resent me?

Barbara That isn't true. I would never do that.

Lucy   Was it because I called her Mummy when I was small instead of you?

Silence.

I know now what that need was. I know what wanted filling. That huge Angela-shaped hole in my heart that opened once you began to turn her away from me. Tell me why Mother. Tell me why. A daughter longs to know these things.

Barbara *throws red wine over* **Lucy**. *Silence.*

Barbara   Oh my darling I'm so sorry.

Lucy   Its okay.

Barbara *takes off her apron gives it to* **Lucy** *to clean herself. She does. They look at each other.*

Lucy   Why?

Barbara   Why?

Lucy   Why?

Barbara   I need love. I need it too.

Silence.

She half-sings.

Barbara   'Don't put your daughter on the stage
Mrs Worthington, don't put your daughter on the stage.'

She laughs to herself. Silence.

Barbara   Noël Coward.

Lucy   Oh.

Barbara   Noël bloody Coward.

Lucy   I love you Mummy.

Barbara   I love you Lucy.

Silence.

I tried to do better with you than I did with your father. I failed with your father. I did all the wrong things.

Silence.

Well after everything, I think we shall both appreciate a break from each other don't you Lucy?

Silence.

Lucy I was thinking of something else.

Barbara Oh?

Silence.

Lucy I don't know if I shall see you again.

Barbara What?

Silence.

Lucy I think if we said I was having a break I would feel honour-bound to. And I don't know what I will do with my life. And apart from the weeks astray in the last couple of years we have spoken every single day of my life and I – And it's so huge. What Angela told me. I feel my whole life has been one fantastical lie. And I have to get away.

Silence.

I have given it consideration and the feeling of dread. Of going away and the knowing that on a certain date I come back. I have to go away and not know.

Barbara I see.

Lucy I think in my own way I've tried before. But somehow the harder I have tried to untangle our – It seems –

Barbara Yes.

Lucy Yes.

Barbara This is all my fault. To think I brought you drugs. I –

Lucy   I don't care about that.

Silence.

But I'm hurt about Daddy. And I must say I'm as cross with Angela as I am with you for not telling me the truth.

Barbara *wipes her eyes. Silence.*

Lucy *looks at her.*

Lucy   All you have ever done is love me and done your best for me. But now I have to go.

Silence.

Lucy   Why didn't you ever talk to us?

Barbara   It's my pain that he died. That I feel he died because of me. I didn't want to burden you both with it.

Lucy   How can a mother's pain ever be a burden to her daughters?

Barbara *wipes her eyes. Silence.*

Lucy   I love you Mummy.

Barbara   I love you Lucy.

Silence.

Lucy   I love you Mummy.

Barbara   I love you Lucy.

Lucy   I love you Mummy.

Barbara   I love you Lucy.

Lucy   I love you Mummy.

Barbara   I love you Lucy.

Silence.

I love you Lucy.

Silence.

I love you Lucy.

Lucy Stop.

Silence.

Stop.

Barbara *wipes her eyes.*

Lucy Don't. I'll.

She wipes her eyes.

Barbara Well. God bless and good luck.

Silence.

Where will you go?

Lucy To South Africa for a couple of months and then – I don't know what.

Barbara How will you –

Lucy Angela has given me some money and a camcorder. To go and see what I can find and have an adventure.

Barbara What an extraordinary girl she is.

Silence.

Lucy Perhaps you will tell her some time.

Silence.

Barbara Yes. I will do my best.

Fourteen

The top of Table Mountain, Cape Town, South Africa.

Lucy *is alone looking out over the ocean towards Robben Island. Silence.*

Oscar *joins her. He is South African.*

Oscar   Can you see Robben Island?

Lucy   Yes.

Oscar   Would you like to go?

Lucy   Perhaps.

Oscar   At one time it was a leper colony. Everyone knows about Nelson Mandela but no one knows about the lepers.

Lucy   Is there an excursion?

Oscar   There's a ferry.

Lucy   Well we should go.

Oscar   You didn't look like you liked the cable car too much?

Lucy   It wasn't too bad. My mother always said I was never good at heights.

They look out at the ocean.

Oscar   That's Lion's Head, that's Signal Hill and that's Devil's Peak.

Lucy   It's quite something here.

Oscar   I never tire of it. No matter how many times.

Lucy   This place is the closet thing to heaven I can imagine. What the fuck is that?

Oscar *laughs.*

Oscar   Oh it's just a dassie. I thought you liked nature?

Lucy Its a rat rabbit with vampire teeth and an evil look in his eye.

She laughs. So does **Oscar**.

Oscar They're all right there's a lot of scraps for them from all the tourists.

Lucy I'm glad I came to South Africa. To the Cape.

Oscar And you didn't come for the football either.

Lucy *laughs.*

Lucy Despite its history, all its difficulties and problems it's a place that's trying to find a new beginning for itself.

She smiles.

Lucy And I get that profoundly.

Oscar So I hear.

They both laugh.

Lucy When I think of my life and being here now I want to cry. Not in a bad way. But I – I'm so pleased I came here.

Oscar *smiles.*

Oscar Well I tell you what Luce I'm sure as shit pleased you did.

Lucy *looks at him and smiles.* **Angela** *comes up onto the high point.*

Oscar Otherwise I never would have met that bloody annoying sister of yours.

Angela *comes towards* **Oscar** *and they kiss for a very long time.*

Angela What's he saying about me Lucylu?

Lucy Oh nothing, he's being boring about Robben Island.

Angela Give him a thump.

Lucy I will.

Oscar   Hey! You wouldn't think she's madly in love with me would you hey Lucy?

Angela   Don't push your luck Oscar or you'll be taking the short way down.

Angela *and* **Oscar** *notice* **Lucy** *looking out at the ocean. They come and stand next to her and look out.*

Lucy   Have you spoken to Mum?

Angela   This morning.

Lucy   How is she?

Angela   Fine.

Lucy   What's she doing?

Angela   She's absolutely fine.

Lucy   Is she?

Angela   I would say so. She's threatening to register on *Guardian* Soulmates.

She shakes her head. **Lucy** *smiles and thinks. Silence.*

Lucy *misses her Mum and blinks back a tear.*

Angela   Are you okay sister?

Lucy   Yes sister.

Angela   Are you sure sister?

Lucy   Yes I am.

Silence.

I think. Perfectly.

She smiles briefly, then thinks, and is filled with a sense of foreboding.

Content. Is the word.

They all look at the ocean.

End of play.

Methuen Drama Student Editions

Jean Anouilh *Antigone* • John Arden *Serjeant Musgrave's Dance*
Alan Ayckbourn *Confusions* • Aphra Behn *The Rover* • Edward Bond
Lear • *Saved* • Bertolt Brecht *The Caucasian Chalk Circle* • *Fear and
Misery in the Third Reich* • *The Good Person of Szechwan* • *Life of Galileo* •
Mother Courage and her Children • *The Resistible Rise of Arturo Ui* • *The
Threepenny Opera* • Anton Chekhov *The Cherry Orchard* • *The Seagull* •
Three Sisters • *Uncle Vanya* • Caryl Churchill *Serious Money* • *Top Girls*
• Shelagh Delaney *A Taste of Honey* • Euripides *Elektra* • *Medea* •
Dario Fo *Accidental Death of an Anarchist* • Michael Frayn *Copenhagen*
• John Galsworthy *Strife* • Nikolai Gogol *The Government Inspector* •
Robert Holman *Across Oka* • Henrik Ibsen *A Doll's House* • *Ghosts* •
Hedda Gabler • Charlotte Keatley *My Mother Said I Never Should* •
Bernard Kops *Dreams of Anne Frank* • Federico García Lorca *Blood
Wedding* • *Doña Rosita the Spinster* (bilingual edition) • *The House of
Bernarda Alba* • (bilingual edition) • *Yerma* (bilingual edition) • David
Mamet *Glengarry Glen Ross* • *Oleanna* • Patrick Marber *Closer* • John
Marston *Malcontent* • Martin McDonagh *The Lieutenant of Inishmore* •
Joe Orton *Loot* • Luigi Pirandello *Six Characters in Search of an Author*
• Mark Ravenhill *Shopping and F***ing* • Willy Russell *Blood Brothers*
• *Educating Rita* • Sophocles *Antigone* • *Oedipus the King* • Wole
Soyinka *Death and the King's Horseman* • Shelagh Stephenson *The
Memory of Water* • August Strindberg *Miss Julie* • J. M. Synge *The
Playboy of the Western World* • Theatre Workshop *Oh What a Lovely
War* Timberlake Wertenbaker *Our Country's Good* • Arnold Wesker
The Merchant • Oscar Wilde *The Importance of Being Earnest* •
Tennessee Williams *A Streetcar Named Desire* • *The Glass Menagerie*

Methuen Drama Modern Plays

include work by

Edward Albee
Jean Anouilh
John Arden
Margaretta D'Arcy
Peter Barnes
Sebastian Barry
Brendan Behan
Dermot Bolger
Edward Bond
Bertolt Brecht
Howard Brenton
Anthony Burgess
Simon Burke
Jim Cartwright
Caryl Churchill
Complicite
Noël Coward
Lucinda Coxon
Sarah Daniels
Nick Darke
Nick Dear
Shelagh Delaney
David Edgar
David Eldridge
Dario Fo
Michael Frayn
John Godber
Paul Godfrey
David Greig
John Guare
Peter Handke
David Harrower
Jonathan Harvey
Iain Heggie
Declan Hughes
Terry Johnson
Sarah Kane
Charlotte Keatley
Barrie Keeffe

Howard Korder
Robert Lepage
Doug Lucie
Martin McDonagh
John McGrath
Terrence McNally
David Mamet
Patrick Marber
Arthur Miller
Mtwa, Ngema & Simon
Tom Murphy
Phyllis Nagy
Peter Nichols
Sean O'Brien
Joseph O'Connor
Joe Orton
Louise Page
Joe Penhall
Luigi Pirandello
Stephen Poliakoff
Franca Rame
Mark Ravenhill
Philip Ridley
Reginald Rose
Willy Russell
Jean-Paul Sartre
Sam Shepard
Wole Soyinka
Simon Stephens
Shelagh Stephenson
Peter Straughan
C. P. Taylor
Theatre Workshop
Sue Townsend
Judy Upton
Timberlake Wertenbaker
Roy Williams
Snoo Wilson
Victoria Wood

Methuen Drama Contemporary Dramatists

include

John Arden (two volumes)
Arden & D'Arcy
Peter Barnes (three volumes)
Sebastian Barry
Dermot Bolger
Edward Bond (eight volumes)
Howard Brenton
  (two volumes)
Richard Cameron
Jim Cartwright
Caryl Churchill (two volumes)
Sarah Daniels (two volumes)
Nick Darke
David Edgar (three volumes)
David Eldridge
Ben Elton
Dario Fo (two volumes)
Michael Frayn (three volumes)
David Greig
John Godber (four volumes)
Paul Godfrey
John Guare
Lee Hall (two volumes)
Peter Handke
Jonathan Harvey
  (two volumes)
Declan Hughes
Terry Johnson (three volumes)
Sarah Kane
Barrie Keeffe
Bernard-Marie Koltès
  (two volumes)
Franz Xaver Kroetz
David Lan
Bryony Lavery
Deborah Levy
Doug Lucie

David Mamet (four volumes)
Martin McDonagh
Duncan McLean
Anthony Minghella
  (two volumes)
Tom Murphy (six volumes)
Phyllis Nagy
Anthony Neilson (two volumes)
Philip Osment
Gary Owen
Louise Page
Stewart Parker (two volumes)
Joe Penhall (two volumes)
Stephen Poliakoff
  (three volumes)
David Rabe (two volumes)
Mark Ravenhill (two volumes)
Christina Reid
Philip Ridley
Willy Russell
Eric-Emmanuel Schmitt
Ntozake Shange
Sam Shepard (two volumes)
Wole Soyinka (two volumes)
Simon Stephens (two volumes)
Shelagh Stephenson
David Storey (three volumes)
Sue Townsend
Judy Upton
Michel Vinaver
  (two volumes)
Arnold Wesker (two volumes)
Michael Wilcox
Roy Williams (three volumes)
Snoo Wilson (two volumes)
David Wood (two volumes)
Victoria Wood

Methuen Drama World Classics

include

Jean Anouilh (two volumes)
Brendan Behan
Aphra Behn
Bertolt Brecht (eight volumes)
Büchner
Bulgakov
Calderón
Čapek
Anton Chekhov
Noël Coward (eight volumes)
Feydeau (two volumes)
Eduardo De Filippo
Max Frisch
John Galsworthy
Gogol
Gorky (two volumes)
Harley Granville Barker
  (two volumes)
Victor Hugo
Henrik Ibsen (six volumes)
Jarry

Lorca (three volumes)
Marivaux
Mustapha Matura
David Mercer (two volumes)
Arthur Miller (six volumes)
Molière
Musset
Peter Nichols (two volumes)
Joe Orton
A. W. Pinero
Luigi Pirandello
Terence Rattigan
  (two volumes)
W. Somerset Maugham
  (two volumes)
August Strindberg
  (three volumes)
J. M. Synge
Ramón del Valle-Inclán
Frank Wedekind
Oscar Wilde

For a complete catalogue
of Methuen Drama titles
write to:

Methuen Drama
50 Bedford square
London WC1B 3DP

or you can visit our website at:

www.methuendrama.com

Printed in the USA
CPSIA information can be obtained
at www.ICGtesting.com
LVHW020843171024
794056LV00002B/373